LEFT TURNS IN BROWN STUDY

WRITING MATTERS! A series edited by
Alexis Pauline Gumbs, Monica Huerta, Erica Rand, and Jerry Zee

LEFT TURNS IN BROWN STUDY

SANDRA RUIZ

DUKE UNIVERSITY PRESS   DURHAM AND LONDON   2024

© 2024 DUKE UNIVERSITY PRESS
All rights reserved

Project Editor: Liz Smith
Designed by Matthew Tauch
Typeset in Archivo Expanded and Degular by Copperline Book Services

Library of Congress Cataloging-in-Publication Data
Names: Ruiz, Sandra, [date] author.
Title: Left turns in brown study / Sandra Ruiz.
Other titles: Writing matters! (Duke University Press)
Description: Durham : Duke University Press, 2024. | Series: Writing matters! | Includes bibliographical references.
Identifiers: LCCN 2023040667 (print)
LCCN 2023040668 (ebook)
ISBN 9781478030126 (paperback)
ISBN 9781478025863 (hardcover)
ISBN 9781478059110 (ebook)
Subjects: LCSH: Grief—Poetry. | Grief in literature. | Minorities in literature. | Postcolonialism in literature. | Literature and race—United States. | American literature—Hispanic American authors—History and criticism. | BISAC: POETRY / American / Hispanic & Latino | LITERARY CRITICISM / Poetry | LCGFT: Poetry.
Classification: LCC PS3618.U547 L44 2024 (print) | LCC PS3618.U547 (ebook) | DDC 810.9/3529—dc23/eng/20240501
LC record available at https://lccn.loc.gov/2023040667
LC ebook record available at https://lccn.loc.gov/2023040668

Cover art: Photo by author.

CONTENTS

THE RETURN (*WHERE WE WERE & WILL BE AGAIN*): AN ENTRY THE PRETURN IF WE WERE DEAD *JUANGO* & ROLAND THE PAST OF AN IMAGE SPLITTING AIR WHERE THE TIMID TAKE THEIR NOSES FOR A WALK MISCARRIED FOR THE PEOPLE FROM THE STARS INNER-CITY JUICE BOXES BLEMISH (*TITLED TWICE*) ACADEMIA DESCENDED: EMANCIPATORY LOVE WORDS AHA! IN FRAGMENTS READING DEBTS TO BE SOFT NECROPOLITICAL FEMINISM LET'S TOUCH INCOMPLETION AS VERSE KIMCHI & TACOS I GUESS I FORGIVE YOU TITLED TWICE (*BLEMISH*) *LAS ELOISAS* WITH JUAN GABRIEL Y CAMILA LONELINESS PROPERTY FOG PLAY SUDDENLY A SENSE BROWN BOYS FOUND IN UNDERTONE FRIENDLESS OOOOOOOOOOOOOO AA: ACADEMIA ASCENDED *LA LUZ* NOT MINE WATCHING DREAMS CON LORD LYDIA TAINTED LIVE WITH A DESK SCORE FOR THE SAND I REMEMBER US TALKING ABOUT LACAN THROUGH J ANYBODY'S ANYBODY THE EARLESS SHARK OR STILL A JANITOR'S KID DECEMBER'S THIRD: THE ENDNOTE FLAWED I'M POSSIBLE TOO OR FLAWED IMPOSSIBLE TO THE FUTURE OF THE FUTURE EPHEMERALITY'S BREEZE EPILOGUES & CIRCLES ALTAR GIRLS *EN FAJARDO* END WITH BIRDS (*ONCE WE ALL FLEW*) UNBODYING GRUNT BASQUIAT'S RIDE MOMENTUM'S SECRET WITH WE TEN SCENES IN GARGOYLES PREMONITIONS: *UNTURNED* THE PRETURN IF WE WERE DEAD *JUANGO* & ROLAND THE PAST OF AN IMAGE SPLITTING AIR WHERE THE TIMID TAKE THEIR NOSES FOR A WALK MISCARRIED FOR THE PEOPLE FROM THE STARS INNER-CITY JUICE BOXES BLEMISH (*TITLED TWICE*) ACADEMIA DESCENDED: EMANCIPATORY LOVE WORDS AHA! IN FRAGMENTS READING DEBTS TO BE SOFT NECROPOLITICAL FEMINISM LET'S TOUCH INCOMPLETION AS VERSE KIMCHI & TACOS I GUESS I FORGIVE YOU TITLED TWICE (*BLEMISH*) *LAS ELOISAS* WITH JUAN GABRIEL Y CAMILA LONELINESS PROPERTY FOG PLAY SUDDENLY A SENSE BROWN BOYS FOUND IN UNDERTONE FRIENDLESS OOOOOOOOOOOOOO AA: ACADEMIA ASCENDED *LA LUZ* NOT MINE WATCHING DREAMS *CON LORD LYDIA* TAINTED LIVE WITH A DESK SCORE FOR THE SAND I REMEMBER US TALKING ABOUT LACAN THROUGH J ANYBODY'S ANYBODY THE EARLESS SHARK OR STILL A JANITOR'S KID DECEMBER'S THIRD: THE ENDNOTE FLAWED I'M POSSIBLE TOO OR FLAWED IMPOSSIBLE TO THE FUTURE

CONTENTS

3	The Return (*where we were & will be again*): An Entry
11	The Preturn
41	If we were dead
42	*Juango* & Roland
45	The Past of an Image
47	Splitting Air
48	Where the Timid Take Their Noses for a Walk
49	Miscarried
53	For the People from the Stars
55	Inner-City Juice Boxes
56	blemish (*titled twice*)
57	Academia Descended: Emancipatory Love Words
58	Aha! in Fragments
59	Reading Debts
63	To Be Soft
64	Necropolitical Feminism
65	Let's Touch
66	Incompletion as Verse
67	Kimchi & Tacos
68	I Guess I Forgive You
71	Titled Twice (*blemish*)
72	*Las Eloisas*
73	With Juan Gabriel y Camila
75	Loneliness Property
76	Fog Play
77	Suddenly a Sense

81	Brown Boys
83	Found in Undertone
85	Friendless
86	OOOOOOOOOOOOOO
87	AA: Academia Ascended
88	*La Luz* Not Mine
91	Watching Dreams *con* Lord Lydia
92	Tainted Live with a Desk
93	Score for the Sand
94	I Remember Us Talking about Lacan through J
95	Anybody's Anybody
97	The Earless Shark or Still a Janitor's Kid
101	December's Third: The Endnote
102	Flawed I'm Possible Too or Flawed Impossible To
103	The Future of the Future
105	Ephemerality's Breeze
106	Epilogues & Circles
108	Altar Girls *en Fajardo*
111	End with Birds (*once we all flew*)
113	Unbodying Grunt
114	Basquiat's Ride
115	Momentum's Secret
118	With We
119	Ten Scenes in Gargoyles
125	Premonitions: *Unturned*

Acknowledgments	131
Bibliography	133

~~TURN~~ TURN TURN TURN TURN TURN TURN TURN TURN
TURN TURN ~~TURN~~ TURN TURN TURN TURN TURN
TURN TURN TURN TURN TURN ~~TURN~~ TURN TURN
TURN ~~TURN~~ TURN TURN TURN TURN TURN TURN
TURN TURN TURN ~~TURN~~ TURN TURN TURN TURN
TURN TURN TURN TURN TURN TURN TURN ~~TURN~~
TURN TURN TURN TURN TURN TURN TURN TURN
TURN TURN ~~TURN~~ TURN TURN TURN TURN TURN
TURN TURN TURN TURN TURN TURN ~~TURN~~ TURN
TURN TURN TURN ~~TURN~~ TURN TURN TURN TURN
TURN ~~TURN~~ TURN TURN TURN TURN TURN TURN
TURN TURN TURN TURN TURN ~~TURN~~ TURN TURN
~~TURN~~ TURN TURN TURN TURN TURN TURN TURN
TURN TURN TURN TURN ~~TURN~~ TURN TURN TURN
TURN TURN ~~TURN~~ TURN TURN TURN TURN TURN
TURN TURN TURN TURN TURN TURN TURN ~~TURN~~
TURN TURN TURN TURN TURN ~~TURN~~ TURN TURN
TURN ~~TURN~~ TURN TURN TURN TURN TURN TURN
TURN TURN TURN ~~TURN~~ TURN TURN TURN TURN
TURN TURN TURN TURN TURN TURN ~~TURN~~ TURN
~~TURN~~ TURN TURN TURN TURN TURN TURN TURN
TURN TURN ~~TURN~~ TURN TURN TURN TURN TURN
TURN TURN TURN TURN ~~TURN~~ TURN TURN TURN
TURN ~~TURN~~ TURN TURN TURN TURN TURN TURN
TURN TURN TURN TURN TURN TURN ~~TURN~~ TURN
TURN TURN TURN ~~TURN~~ TURN TURN TURN TURN
TURN TURN TURN TURN TURN ~~TURN~~ TURN TURN
~~TURN~~ TURN TURN TURN TURN TURN TURN TURN
TURN TURN TURN TURN TURN TURN TURN ~~TURN~~
TURN TURN TURN ~~TURN~~ TURN TURN TURN TURN
~~TURN~~ TURN TURN TURN TURN TURN TURN TURN
TURN TURN TURN TURN TURN ~~TURN~~ TURN TURN
TURN TURN ~~TURN~~ TURN TURN TURN TURN TURN
TURN TURN TURN TURN TURN TURN TURN ~~TURN~~

THE RETURN (*WHERE WE WERE & WILL BE AGAIN*): AN ENTRY

Every day, year (any date)
During the early morning (some time)

I've been returning with the dead since I can remember listening.

Readings & writings that moved past any alphabetic entry into the sonic refrain—what kinds of sounds muster life across a chorus of energies, desires for returning? I've been returning since I sensed my father couldn't use paper & pen to weaponize against oppression, not because he wasn't "educated," but unschooled. Trained in the modifications of street verse & the will to return to that place & time & thought that might release him from being unread, unknown, unheard, he spoke with spirits & there was listening.

Left Turns in Brown Study was written aloud, for & with them, for & with listening.

I often read to him, turning the pages between languages, countries & dreams; you know, letters, notes, street signs, medical forms, unrequited hiring ambitions & memories of mothers, motherlands—there were always stories to be retold to one day be returned. That is to say that I learned that any type of study would require the embrace of spirits & ghosts (his & all of mine) for anything learned, written, shared, belonged only tangentially to me; mostly everything was his, theirs.

The colonial world has been calling them *the dead*, but the dead are always living powerfully within the confines of empires.

Study, then, leaves one (*to be left, to be left*) in an ongoing Brown meditation, a nonlinear suffering that is also the kindness of liberation & life returned in citation. Unlike my ancestors, who were not granted the luxury to spend days dropped into gloomy intellectual embrace, I learned to use written words to mobilize worlds, mostly from sounds, mostly from them.

Just because ghosts & spirits refuse print does not mean they refuse syllables.

I heard everything. I heard everything I saw in aura. I heard everything I felt across bodies. We heard them. We wrote them. We listened. This book is written from the ear, from their sounds to all of mine, in the intricate intervals of conjoined scores.

Left Turns in Brown Study mourns the dead as study & understands study as an ongoing death that prospers in citational turns. The collection oscillates between poetry & theory into the worlding/wordings of Brownness, synchronic shifts in feeling, thinking, being, grieving, acting, doing, reading, writing, sensing, listening that suggest, in returning, one uncovers the promise of studying together.

Always alive, always awaiting the moment to be enacted, returns are visceral responses, sometimes rejections for reconsideration, investment & always intentional movements in reciprocity that go back to give back to get back, disappear to reappear, implying *where we were and will be again*. An entry re(turn)ed.

Left Turns in Brown Study, written for & with a chosen symphony of ghosts & spirits, follows the call & response of all sorts of death that lead one through litanies of loss, mourning rituals & the spiraling cages of modes of difference. Working from within theory & activism by mostly Black & Brown thinkers, the text attempts to link several concepts as an entangled operation: brown study as connected to Brownness, Brownness as always a type of liberatory mourning, the turn as an ideological, political & intellectual heuristic, learning as ongoing grief & grievance, writing as citational death/life & the typographical-turn-page as a new methodology for signaling emancipatory directives in study.

The poems, theory fragments, endnotes, lyrical essays, entries, letters & typographical-turn-pages across this collection bridge brown study & Brownness by presenting the theoretical apparatus of the turn—turns we make in thinking, reading, writing & study—including, but not limited to, a Brown type of study that turns to citation to call forward a series of minoritarian energies that reframe archival repositories. In doing so, each turn left offers Brownness as a practice of engagement, for harboring loss & its possibility for more abundant ways of living together more queerly. *Left Turns* is invested in utopia, queer possibility, poetics & the fluid communities these forms hail.

From belated mentors to illiterate ancestors to victims of colonial violence across institutional sites, including instructional spaces, to following the politics of spiritual logic, *Left Turns* grapples with all types of institutional grief, grievance & giving(s), or the ways we learn to carry these legacies as minoritarian subjects of/with the dead in constant acts of mourning.

The poems, divided into sections by typographical-turn-pages, directly engage one another to reorder, reject, revitalize, reconsider, recognize (in style & content) the colonial mandates of gender, sexuality, race, nation, family, territory, class, literacy & learning by traveling across time in form & formatting. Sections of poems, marked by typographical-turn-pages, hold the reader's hand, asking them to turn left to turn into a sound, phrase, idea, to connect the syllables into meanings for anticolonial ways of reading, writing, listening, mourning.

These left turns move in counterclockwise fashion to reorient the dominant circular motions of time & space. But these left turns can also be perilous, requiring the reader to intentionally move with & through blind spots, a way of reading that doesn't privilege sight, but reorders it. Repeated lines, words, sounds, phrases, verses, throughout the volume, redirect the reader to fundamental rhythms of listening again in doing study.

As the reader turns, *their left turns* work to also suggest that all modes of difference are categories of & vessels for mourning.

Everything foundationally presented as indexically stable, for example race, contains the vestiges of loss, an ongoing return to returning through citational practice & politic. The category's inherent instability rattles the human condition & the poems attempt to resuscitate breath. For in every passing breath we gather for one another in choreographed repetition—a respired turn in returning.

Perhaps our intentional desire to be together exceeds the demise of death as the aftermath of living. Perhaps we can find one another in the turn to return, in the citational politics that render forgotten Brown lives beautiful and meaningful. Brownness, for instance, operates as an ongoing homage that does not merely exist in negation, excess & lack, but across immaterial lingerings that manifest energies always already energizing. Brownness is not only a relational or comparative construction, but an entangled orchestration, joined to other floating & changing modes of difference, which include layers of loss imposed by & built from institutional & educational infrastructure.

So, what can the turn to, not the turn away, provide us as readers, thinkers, studiers & inevitably always already mourners? What if Brownness is just a turn? A return to study?[1] What would it mean to return, not as an injured attachment, but an act of deliberate study? A return to the loss that turns again? What does turning left manifest, uphold in reality & fantasy, warrant in social politics & how do these left turns leave us with what's left to handle & maybe burn?

Even ashes remain in plentiful reminder to remind us of what is to return. So, if we must perpetually mourn, let's not do it alone. If we must write of mourning, let's not elaborate singularly. If we must turn into something, some thought, let us turn left together, not away from one another. If we must return to Brown study, let's turn to the sounding crevasses of Brownness as precision, an iterative listening across ensembles of genre like poetic form, theory & criticism. For no matter how it is reproduced, Brownness is always citation.[2]

1. Turn to "The Preturn" for how this kind of study is enacted in a lyrical essay marking ghosts, spirits, ideas, schools of thought & dialogues between thinkers.

2. The repetition of certain words is called upon by the spirits. When we write, think & cite, we participate in a form of death making that is essentially life affirming. We recall that energies, entities, ideas exist infinitely in citation. The spirits share the following (in paraphrase): repetition is a preplanned ritual, a refrain resung; in saying/citing one is incapable of not returning to one another. (What if we can't?) Put out your hands, palms up & receive the turn.

tUrn tUrn tUrn tUrn tUrn tUrn tUrn tUrn tUrn tUrn tUrn tUrn
tUrn tUrn tUrn tUrn tUrn tUrn tUrn tUrn tUrn tUrn tUrn tUrn
tUrn tUrn tUrn tUrn tUrn tUrn tUrn tUrn tUrn tUrn tUrn tUrn
tUrn tUrn tUrn tUrn tUrn tUrn tUrn tUrn tUrn tUrn tUrn tUrn
tUrn tUrn tUrn tUrn tUrn tUrn tUrn tUrn tUrn tUrn tUrn tUrn
tUrn tUrn tUrn tUrn tUrn tUrn tUrn tUrn tUrn tUrn tUrn tUrn
tUrn tUrn tUrn tUrn tUrn tUrn tUrn tUrn tUrn tUrn tUrn tUrn
tUrn tUrn tUrn tUrn tUrn tUrn tUrn tUrn tUrn tUrn tUrn tUrn
tUrn tUrn tUrn tUrn tUrn tUrn tUrn tUrn tUrn tUrn tUrn tUrn
tUrn tUrn tUrn tUrn tUrn tUrn tUrn tUrn tUrn tUrn tUrn tUrn
tUrn tUrn tUrn tUrn tUrn tUrn tUrn tUrn tUrn tUrn tUrn tUrn
tUrn tUrn tUrn tUrn tUrn tUrn tUrn tUrn tUrn tUrn tUrn tUrn
tUrn tUrn tUrn tUrn tUrn tUrn tUrn tUrn tUrn tUrn tUrn tUrn
tUrn tUrn tUrn tUrn tUrn tUrn tUrn tUrn tUrn tUrn tUrn tUrn
tUrn tUrn tUrn tUrn tUrn tUrn tUrn tUrn tUrn tUrn tUrn tUrn
tUrn tUrn tUrn tUrn tUrn tUrn tUrn tUrn tUrn tUrn tUrn tUrn
tUrn tUrn tUrn tUrn tUrn tUrn tUrn tUrn tUrn tUrn tUrn tUrn
tUrn tUrn tUrn tUrn tUrn tUrn tUrn tUrn tUrn tUrn tUrn tUrn
tUrn tUrn tUrn tUrn tUrn tUrn tUrn tUrn tUrn tUrn tUrn tUrn
tUrn tUrn tUrn tUrn tUrn tUrn tUrn tUrn tUrn tUrn tUrn tUrn
tUrn tUrn tUrn tUrn tUrn tUrn tUrn tUrn tUrn tUrn tUrn tUrn
tUrn tUrn tUrn tUrn tUrn tUrn tUrn tUrn tUrn tUrn tUrn tUrn
tUrn tUrn tUrn tUrn tUrn tUrn tUrn tUrn tUrn tUrn tUrn tUrn
tUrn tUrn tUrn tUrn tUrn tUrn tUrn tUrn tUrn tUrn tUrn tUrn
tUrn tUrn tUrn tUrn tUrn tUrn tUrn tUrn tUrn tUrn tUrn tUrn
tUrn tUrn tUrn tUrn tUrn tUrn tUrn tUrn tUrn tUrn tUrn tUrn
tUrn tUrn tUrn tUrn tUrn tUrn tUrn tUrn tUrn tUrn tUrn tUrn

THE PRETURN

I've been writing for
my father since the day I
learned to read, or the day I
imagined he couldn't.
Alphabets passed on to
others, mothers, sisters, not
him. I followed the movement
of speak and listen, a railroad
aboveground within meters
from consonants to touch.[1]
Illiteracy is both a colonial &
ancestral phenomenon; the
body carries and passes it
through—next of kin.[2]
The living shoulder it;
the living-as-
shapeless share it, the
formless remodify its
contours, especially
when words are
spoken-read.

Through the silent-
violent storms of those non-
reading pages, some entity
learns to read, write, offer
meaning to long consumed
histories. Sometimes
reading happens through
the tongue of that tongue

onto the space of someone schooled outside of school.

This kind of reading opens the library to the schoolyard, the block across the fence. That block, our block, is where study meets the ephemeral lingering & longing of existences, a reading-in-one-as-common. But it is also where study, when given up to the moods of structure, imperial conditioning, and militarization, leaves the studier in the synapses of mourning, where the grief held is the grievance[3] never filed[4] but instead, internally buried to continually resurrect.

That is to share that every condition is also every instruction for becoming-with, against, through the institutional spasms and mandates of race, gender, sexuality, class, ethnicity, -ability, often categories used to perform identification while holding tightly to the very death that organizes these pre-conditioned performances.[5] These modes of difference that we labor to protect, uphold, project, be & become are also forms of mourning that are not dissimilar to how one experiences lost objects, subjects, entities. The illusion of category eventually dies, eventually reinvents.

Personally & communally, we mourn the institutions that fail us & that we also fail, for we can never become that one image, turned copy, made by infrastructure & a million times reproduced and circulated as representative of you, me, them, us-all.

In these interlaced mourning rituals, we might attend to how modes of difference & grief rely on conjoined processes, similar structural measures that express how every group of identification is already a collected collection for death. One can never exist as sexual & racial montage, for one is already contrived into the single frame.[6]

So how does a subject move "from being a

subject of grief to being a subject of grievance"?[7] Cheng's *The Melancholy of Race* is a preemptive performativity of race that operates in relation, consent, consequence, refusal, & force. We "swallow" the grievance as deep loss in our continual grieving of it, you, them, her, him, us-all.[8] How do we expel this protracted mourning in contempt of indexicality, facticity, conformation, and promises of freedom, or is it the promise of relief?

Left Turns in Brown Study is a book about continuous loss, rigorous love, melancholic disdain, introjected institutional grievance, political pain, social redemption, anticolonial sentiment in form & content—all parts in active nonlinear grief & provoked by a hopeful & meditative sadness. Like the idiom brown study—a gloomy, reclusive, abstracted meditation of thought[9]— this book conjures the dreadful scenes of those no longer present in form & the desire to return anew to what has passed, what could have been, alongside the desire to let live again through verse, rhyme, word, syllable punctuation, citation, emotional tendencies, affective voids & the play/playfulness between forming content & deforming organization.[10]

Left Turns is also about letting one relive in the space of dark & dismal minor keys; for in doing so, one sounds out alternative cartographies[11] & maybe galaxies for being-together, even if often done in interior discomforting contagion.

In tune with the political logics of Brown thought & Brownness across theorists & creatives, *Left Turns in Brown Study* is somber, quietly riotous, at times dreamingly depressing in abysmal displeasure & indignant rumination for greater presence & futures, where mourning meets difference in the folds of their entwined orchestrations.

If every category for being is always already an oppressive system for not being, then *Left Turns* asks the reader to engage the inter-articulations of brown study & brownness, to think again about Brown thought as happening now, here, then, there, again, a with & alongside, a before & always in some after, too. If there is Brown thought,[12] there is brown reading, brown folk, brown feelings, brown embodiment, brown kinesthetics, brown material bodies, brown sight, brown touch, brown ensembles, brown entanglements, brown as in knotted, brown as in curious study, brown as in turning, brown as in turning left, or left turning.

In making turns, I shift to thinkers & their work on brownness. For instance, José Esteban Muñoz's decades-long[13] contemplation of this term & its connection to negative affect, negation as subject formation, incompletion as a productive force, being-together through being a problem & queer & brown utopic aspirations.[14] From the transmission of brownness[15] to brown worldings[16] & feeling brown[17] to the sense of brown, to brown as wise,[18] bestiary,[19] vulnerable,[20] wild,[21] & politically problematic,[22] to brown as an "homage to the history of brown power,"[23] a diasporic political porosity across time & space, to brownness as an "apartness together"[24] in ensemblic abjections, or brown as a "swarm of singularities,"[25] to a brown commons as a movement, a transient export,[26] Muñoz envisions past how "color colors thoughts"[27] & negotiates how the conditions of coloring spawn worlds—some here, some still in transfiguration, but always in remembrance of the fact that the "world is not becoming brown; rather, it has been brown."[28]

A brown commons, then, is now, here, there; never removed & from fugitive study.[29] It is in line with the unruly contours of Harney's & Moten's undercommons, or a "refuge colony" in the "downlow" or "where the work gets subverted,"[30] where labor is always done in "unsafe neighborhoods"[31] in maroon operation outside corporate mandates & tacit policies for cooperating.

This brown commons engages the social & legal vulnerabilities & violences that mitigate brown life in the everyday with and against "property, finance, and to capital's overarching mechanisms of domination."[32] These commons embrace the "illegalities of

Brownness."[33] That is to say that if brown feelings transform social and cultural engagements and "pave the way toward a more egalitarian and utopic future, then the feelings of 'illegal' brown subjects have the potential to radically alter sociality in an antibrown world by visualizing and sounding out a future that is not entrenched in an aberration of democracy."[34] Rather, brownness, as also an "otherwiseness," is rooted in a more "subterranean route to the production of knowledge"[35] through sensing & feeling, through brown worlding, group sharing, methexis, precisely within the racial & colonial confines of national, cultural, economic injustice & disparity.[36] That is to also share that the brown commons is a nomadic site of exchange & contact where brownness is activated by "embodied politics"[37] that vary & turn according to situation & the historical markers that inform future flows in ensemble. Or "to understand a map is to shrink the world; to plan; to color" across entangled embodiments.[38]

By way of illegalities, incoherencies, incompletions, the unmanageable of management, *Left Turns in Brown Study* also hopes to prosper in the "intramural,"[39] the "unofficial,"[40] the "feral,"[41] the unquiet silences of sonic incommunicability,[42] alongside the "castaways,"[43] the "motley crews,"[44] the "renegades,"[45] the "maroons"[46] through an "aesthetics of excess," [47] an "inheritance of haunting," echoes of "brown baby lullabies,"[48] and "brown neon"[49] vitalities for those who read, or non-read differently, off the page in multiple line-break-sounds & breaths against written words, literate social scenes, and legal worlds.

Brownness is movement, abundance, outflow, off-course with & without metered pace. "To think about brownness is to accept that it arrives at us";[50] we work to semi-attune to its measures in an ongoing process of locating our collective communions. Therefore, Brownness is "about contact," not only about being with, but "being alongside."[51] A type of touch that activates plenitude, motion, operation, mobility & motility.[52] It is an impetus to navigate past individualization into the space of simultaneous multi-presences & multiverses that are always already alive & running off course.[53] Or, Brownness may have always already been a "postcolonial love poem."[54]

In this sense, Brownness exceeds the parameters of its own incompletion, as it performs in shifting references on & off grids, pages & spectrums.[55] As Nitasha Tamar Sharma confirms of brownness: "racial formation is an always incomplete process of contestation and negotiation, of hegemony and resistance, and of imposition and adoption," or brown "sticks around"[56] as it also "swerves of matter, organic and otherwise"[57] spilling past the impulse to contain its inorganic individualization.

These swerves, rotations, turns, shifts into movements might fall in line with what fahima ife calls the "anachoreography" of black study or "the feral spirit of study"[58] where choreographic scores realign in wayward steps to drop into motion across tameless movements. Anachoreography is both a methodology & practice that requires "stammering, and moving again inside our quiet, entangled, pneumatic intimacies."[59] Turning to the undercommons as well, ife calls for a maroon choreography or an endeavor to account for black study "as something otherwise, some wiser configuration other than an argument."[60] Like Muñoz's brownness as other(wise)ness, ife's choreographic-poetic-theory-scores address the steps we take toward the anti-corporate finish line—no one, at least not in otherwise, from the otherwise, waits for the untamed to become democratically domesticated.

Against state strategy, study, like Harney and Moten note, "happens in hiding."[61] Perhaps in the quiet left turns that in evolving resurrect those hidden spaces for multi-voices in queer sounds;[62] queer not as in who we bang but how we deliberately breathe;[63] to deliver a whisper-scream past the gates that scold & refuse to pardon the beautiful deviants that in just being, dreaming-together, rescue us from the doldrums of oppressive mediocrity & social obedience.

Left Turns in Brown Study, written across temporal voices & ages, for & with a symphony of ghosts & spirits, invites the reader to make sharp, arbitrary, driven turns on & across the page through time & space. It requires a "sustained antiphony"[64] between us, them, the material & immaterial worlds, words, negative space, between cuts

& sounds that call forth harmonies in dissonance & assonance in polyrhythms.

Left Turns is an invitation to turn back to turn forward to turn left again & return—for the swivel redirects the ungovernable route.

To intentionally say when studying: "I turn to," "I turn away from," "this turn marks," or "to turn to this theory signifies" all designate intellectual & ideological direction, a rotation in thought that spins a movement but also a relationship with others,[65] a relationship with other ideas, maybe a little deadened upon creation but reborn upon circulation, utterance, reiteration.

Sometimes conjoined & other times random fixations that become logic through poetic verse, *Left Turns in Brown Study* peels the heart visible into segments for her, him, you, them, us—all in whichever direction mourning claims the sentiment, by working through the haunted communions of relation & brownness[66] that linger of energy, ideas, life forces & life memories.

For instance, a left turn in speech is often uninhibited, indiscriminate, an incidental idea made off track, a turned unconscious trick that unveils the protected privacies of thinking, reading, writing. How can we theorize this turn as a politically charged non-infrastructure? How do we deliberately welcome revolve & change into & with the turn? How do we turn—like the living dead or the dead-alive—into countermeasures toward the brutality of everyday loss, everyday cultural illiteracy?

Why turn left? What does the Left historically indicate, obfuscate, lift, empower, and recharge? To mark the left, here & again, but to also know that one can be left, everything leaves to be enlivened via the multi-functionality of turning, turning left, turning into and from the abject, *sucias* & all those bad bitches to the left, to the left.[67]

Likewise, the idiom brown study deserves another turn here. Searching for the etymology of this phrase & its connection to brownness, Chon A. Noriega disentangles the words *brown* & *study* to share something about the contours of being brown. Juxtaposing the words *melancholy* & *brown*,[68] he discloses how colors shelter histories but are always inherently multilayered. He traces the term *brown study* to a book published in 1532, which in announcing the idiom conveys this rationale for its usage: "lack of company will soon lead a man into a brown study."[69] To be led into, not necessarily by one's volition but an energetic force that compels the subject into a feeling of doom & gloom, is the condition of brown study.

First cited in the sixteenth century, the term describes "a state of intense, sometimes melancholy reverie."[70] It is a position of being that arises from a combination of colors that comprise brown (red, green, or orange & blue, or yellow or purple); a spectrum of colors & a metaphor for racial mixture,[71] not a stationary or stable identity marker[72] but one that exceeds the dialectics of racial formation & designation; & subsequently welcomes encounter, exchange, flows into otherwise ways of being upon touch, crossing, falling, talking, being, doing things together as together.

While depicted as a dark mood occurring in reclusive thoughts, the term resurfaces in the nineteenth century as a powerful enveloping emotional condition.[73] Not just a condition of being that one is led into, but one that a subject falls into, a descension into brown study. Thus, one is not guided by some mythical entity into this kind of study but pushed into the gloomy condition. A desolate contemplation, a lonely despair that takes over the subject, that the subject almost collapses into, that supernaturally thrusts the body into a state of anguish, heartache, bleakness. To be pushed from one axis point into movement, a pivot, a turn.

Could it be that deliberate and rigorous study is always an act of sorrow; could all contemplative study be brown then? Could brown be the study? Could study, as in everything is alive but ending in ongoing citation, be a form of mourning that is also a form of brown study that lands us in the perpetual constructions of brownness?[74]

Study is an aggrieved force—belonging to anyone, anything, figure, spirit or otherwise, until some meaning-feeling is inferred, attached to the entity & offers breath; shared conspiration. Study is respiration in mourning: several parts reclusive recursive; many parts fleeting like the immaterial energy in constant returns.

In *Left Turns in Brown Study* there are ghosts & there are spirits. Ghosts remain to rethink their presence—neither here nor totally there; they linger sometimes regretfully.[75] Spirits pass on & through & return to re-return. They remind us to be something other than a move into a passing, passing on.[76] Both can be playful. Both can guide. Both carry memory—theirs, ours, our entangled pleasures, illusions, and afflictions.[77]

Left Turns in Brown Study is a book to be read by them & written with them. They are the reader & the cowriter, everything made today for all yesterdays into all futures that remind us that to turn is to live again... differently.

Left Turns in Brown Study assumes

that everything is already almost dead, but dead as in alive & in motion, magnetic fields that recharge energies into ongoing non-stillness.[78] For nothing stays still even if dropped into a brown study—even drops reverberate, slick bounces in the time it takes to turn a phrase & re-turn study.[79]

Every poem across these pages is an offering, a lamenting, a returning to a scene to move forward in precise, citational listening.[80] Every poem is an institutional studies turned study, a loss & their let goes, grievance introjected into memory & held in archive for the shapeless, you, her, him, them, us-all, like words to a hit & syllables to a listener—in reminder, we remain.

1. Whitehead, *Making Love with the Land*, 87.
   WHITEHEAD, IN THEIR CHAPTER "WRITING AS A RUPTURE," DISCUSSES THE SIGNIFICANCE OF ORAL TRADITION AS A TYPE OF WRITING. THEY STATE, "ORALITY IS REALITY" (87).

2. R. T. Rodríguez, *Next of Kin*.
   SEE R. T. RODRÍGUEZ FOR MORE ON KINSHIP FORMATIONS.

3. Cheng, *The Melancholy of Race*, 3.
   SEE CHENG FOR MORE ON SUBJECTS OF GRIEF TO SUBJECTS OF GRIEVANCE AND THE RELATIONSHIP BETWEEN TERMS.

4. Ahmed, *Complaint!*, 3.
   SEE AHMED FOR MORE ON THE FORMALITIES OF FILING COMPLAINTS THAT INCLUDE THE ONES UNFILED AS WELL. I AM THINKING OF SARA AHMED HERE IN CONNECTION TO ANNE ANLIN CHENG'S WORK ON GRIEF AS GRIEVANCE.

5. Jaime, *The Queer Nuyorican*.
   Montez, *Keith Haring's Line*.
   L. Gutiérrez, *Performing Mexicanidad*.
   Rivera-Servera, *Performing Queer Latinidad*.
   SEE JAIME, MONTEZ, L. GUTIÉRREZ, AND RIVERA-SERVERA FOR MORE ON THE INTRICACIES AND COMPLEXITIES OF QUEER LATINX IDENTIFICATION AND PERFORMANCE.

6. McMillan, *Embodied Avatars*, 7–11.
   SEE URI MCMILLAN'S MASTERFUL WORK ON BLACK WOMEN'S POWERFUL SELF-OBJECTION ACROSS PERFORMANCE ART AS A COUNTERMEASURE TO ART HISTORICAL AND COLONIAL LOGICS THAT OFTEN FRAME MINORITARIAN SUBJECTS ONLY THROUGH THE LENS OF OBJECTHOOD.

7. Cheng, *The Melancholy of Race*, 3.
   I'VE BEEN RETURNING TO CHENG'S BRILLIANT ANALYSES OF GRIEF AND GRIEVANCE AND THE WAYS IN WHICH THEY BOTH STRUCTURE THE INTERNALIZATION OF THE PERFORMATIVITY OF RACE.

8. Cheng, *The Melancholy of Race*, 8.
   SEE CHENG FOR MORE ON THE "SWALLOWING" OF GRIEF AND GRIEVANCES.

9. Stein, "Golden Brown."
   SEE STEIN FOR MORE ON "BROWN STUDY" AND HOW IT MIGHT HAVE FALLEN OUT OF FASHION.

10. Ruiz and Vourloumis, *Formless Formation*, 9–15.
    THE ENTIRE BOOK MOVES ACROSS NINE WORDS IN A SERIES OF VIGNETTES TO ENACT THE DEFORMING OF FORM ACROSS THE TEXT.

11   Vazquez, *Listening in Detail*, 19.
SEE VAZQUEZ FOR MORE ABOUT SOUND AS NEW WORLD MAKING THROUGH THE POWER OF LISTENING ACUTELY FOR THE DETAILS THAT RENDER WORLDS ACROSS HISTORICAL AND SONIC LANDSCAPES.

12   Rodriguez, "The Brown Study."
SEE RODRIGUEZ FOR ANOTHER TAKE ON BROWN STUDY.

13   JOSÉ ESTEBAN MUÑOZ BEGINS THEORIZING BROWNNESS, IDEOLOGY, AND AFFECT IN HIS FIRST BOOK—*DISIDENTIFICATIONS*—AND CONTINUES TO DO SO AS HE MOVES THROUGH CONSIDERATIONS OF QUEERNESS AND RACE IN *CRUISING UTOPIA*, TO THEN RETURN TO THEIR INTERARTICULATION IN *SENSE OF BROWN*. THESE THREE BOOKS, WHILE SINGULAR CONSTRUCTIONS, CAN ALSO BE READ AS A TRILOGY OF THOUGHT THAT WORKS TO UNDO THE SEPARATIONS OF DIFFERENCE THROUGH THE AESTHETIC.

14   Muñoz, *Disidentifications*.
Muñoz, *Cruising Utopia*.
Muñoz, *The Sense of Brown*.
SEE MUÑOZ ACROSS THESE THREE TEXTS FOR A SENSE OF HOW BROWNNESS TRANSFORMS, SETTLES AND UNSETTLES CATEGORIES OF IDENTIFICATION.

15   Muñoz, "'Chico, What Does It Feel Like to Be a Problem?': The Transmission of Brownness," in *The Sense of Brown*, 36.
SEE MUÑOZ FOR MORE ON BROWNNESS AS TRANSMISSION.

16   Muñoz, "Brown Worldings: José Rodríguez-Soltero, Tania Bruguera, and María Irene Fornés," in *The Sense of Brown*, 118.
SEE MUÑOZ FOR MORE ON BROWN WORLDINGS.

17   Muñoz, "Feeling Brown: Ethnicity and Affect in Ricardo Bracho's *The Sweetest Hangover (and Other STDs)*," in *The Sense of Brown*, 8.
SEE MUÑOZ FOR MORE ON FEELING BROWN.

18   Muñoz, "Wise Latinas," in *The Sense of Brown*, 100.
SEE MUÑOZ FOR MORE ON WISE LATINAS.

19   Muñoz, "Performing the Bestiary: Carmelita Tropicana's *With What Ass Does the Cockroach Sit? / Con Que Culo se Sienta la Cucaracha?*," in *The Sense of Brown*, 78.
SEE MUÑOZ FOR MORE ON PERFORMING THE BESTIARY.

20   Muñoz, "The Vulnerability Artist: Nao Bustamante and the Sad Beauty of Reparation," in *The Sense of Brown*, 47.
SEE MUÑOZ FOR MORE ON VULNERABILITY.

21   Muñoz, "The Sense of *Wildness*: The Brown Commons after Paris Burned," in *The Sense of Brown*, 128.
SEE MUÑOZ FOR MORE ON WILDNESS.

22 Muñoz, "'Chico, What Does It Feel Like to Be a Problem?': The Transmission of Brownness," in *The Sense of Brown*, 36.
SEE MUÑOZ FOR MORE ON BEING POLITICALLY PROBLEMATIC.

23 Muñoz, "The Brown Commons," in *The Sense of Brown*, 3.
SEE MUÑOZ FOR MORE ON BROWNNESS AS AN HOMAGE TO THE HISTORY OF BROWN POWER.

24 Muñoz, "'Chico, What Does It Feel Like to Be a Problem?': The Transmission of Brownness," in *The Sense of Brown*, 39.
SEE MUÑOZ FOR MORE ON BROWNNESS AS AN "APARTNESS TOGETHER."

25 Muñoz, *The Sense of Brown*, 149.
SEE MUÑOZ FOR MORE ON BROWNNESS AS A "SWARM OF SINGULARITIES." THE DELIBERATE SPECIFIC CITATIONAL WORK ABOVE ATTEMPTS TO SHOW HOW MUÑOZ PROVIDED AMPLE WAYS OF SENSING BROWNNESS; NEVER A MYOPIC CONSTRUCTION, BROWNNESS ITSELF IS A SHAPE-SHIFTER, TAKING ON NEW TERMS AND MEANINGS THAT WHILE INDIVIDUAL LIVE IN CONJUNCTION AND REMAIN THROUGH CITATION.

26 Muñoz, "The Brown Commons," in *The Sense of Brown*, 2.
SEE MUÑOZ FOR MORE ON BROWNNESS AS MOVEMENT.

27 Rodriguez, "The Brown Study," 119.
SEE RODRIGUEZ FOR MORE ON HOW COLOR ITSELF ADDS HUES TO THOUGHT.

28 Muñoz, *The Sense of Brown*, 3.
MUÑOZ SHOWS THAT THINKING THROUGH A BROWN COMMONS SUGGESTS THAT THE WORLD HAS BEEN BROWN RATHER THAN IT IS JUST BECOMING BROWN.

29 Harney and Moten, "The University and the Undercommons," in *The Undercommons*, 28.
SEE HARNEY AND MOTEN FOR MORE ON FUGITIVE STUDY.

30 Harney and Moten, "The University and the Undercommons," in *The Undercommons*, 26.
SEE HARNEY AND MOTEN FOR MORE ON REFUGE COLONIES, THE DOWNLOW, AND OTHER SITES WHERE THE WORK GETS SUBVERTED.

31 Harney and Moten, "The University and the Undercommons," in *The Undercommons*, 28.
SEE HARNEY AND MOTEN FOR MORE ON THE LABOR DONE IN UNSAFE NEIGHBORHOODS.

32 Muñoz, *The Sense of Brown*, 3.
SEE MUÑOZ FOR MORE ON THE VIOLENCE THAT MITIGATES BROWN LIFE IN THE EVERYDAY WITH AND AGAINST PROPERTY, FINANCE, AND CAPITAL'S OVERARCHING MECHANISMS OF DOMINATION.

33 García, "The Illegalities of Brownness," 103.
SEE GARCÍA FOR MORE ON ILLEGALITIES AND BROWN SUBJECTIVITIES.

34 García, "The Illegalities of Brownness," 103.
SEE GARCÍA FOR MORE ON THE POTENTIAL OF ILLEGAL BROWN SUBJECTS TO RADICALLY ALTER SOCIALITY IN AN ANTIBROWN WORLD.

35 Muñoz, *The Sense of Brown*, 101.
SEE MUÑOZ FOR MORE ON BROWNNESS AS "AN OTHERWISENESS" AND THE POTENTIAL FOR THE PRODUCTION OF SUBTERRANEAN ROUTES FOR THE PRODUCTION OF KNOWLEDGE.

36 Guzmán, "Brown," 25.
JAVIER JOSHUA GUZMÁN SMARTLY ASKS, "WHAT KARMIC, THOUGH NOT NECESSARILY PUNITIVE, LOGIC DISCLOSES ITSELF IN BROWNNESS?" AND SHARES THAT BROWN "AMBIGUOUSLY SIGNALS UNITY AND DISTINCTION."

37 Musser, "Sensing Brownness," 48–49.
SEE MUSSER FOR MORE ON EMBODIED POLITICS.

38 Villarreal, "A Field of Onions: Brown Study," stanza 6.
FOR MORE ON THE BEAUTY OF POET VILLARREAL'S RENDERING OF BROWN STUDY THROUGH VERSE, READ THE TWENTY-SEVEN-VERSE POEM.

39 Muñoz, *The Sense of Brown*, 4.
SEE MUÑOZ FOR MORE ON BROWNNESS AS INTRAMURAL.

40 Muñoz, *The Sense of Brown*, 4.
SEE MUÑOZ FOR MORE ON THE UNOFFICIAL AND UNOFFICIALITY.

41 ife, *Maroon Choreography*, ix, 27.
SEE IFE FOR MORE ON THE FERAL AS POLITICAL DISSENSUS.

42 Crawley, "Tongues," in *Blackpentecostal Breath*, 197.
SEE HOW ASHON CRAWLEY DEPLOYS AESTHETIC POSSIBILITY THROUGH BREATH AND SOUND IN *BLACKPENTECOSTAL BREATH*.

43 Harney and Moten, *The Undercommons*, 29.
SEE HARNEY AND MOTEN FOR MORE ON CASTAWAYS.

44 Harris, "Introduction," in *Experiments in Exile*, 2–8.
SEE HARRIS FOR A MORE ROBUST THEORIZATION OF THE MOTLEY CREW.

45 Harney and Moten, *The Undercommons*, 29.
SEE HARNEY AND MOTEN FOR MORE ON RENEGADES AND RENEGADE SUBJECTIVITIES.

46 Harney and Moten, *The Undercommons*.
ife, *Maroon Choreography*, ix, 27.
IFE'S WORK IS IN DIRECT DIALOGUE WITH *THE UNDERCOMMONS*, SPECIFICALLY WITH THE TERM *MAROON*, USED TO RECHOREOGRAPH BOTH BLACK LIFE AND BLACK STUDY.

47 Hernandez, "Introduction," in *Aesthetics of Excess*, 11.
SEE JILLIAN HERNANDEZ'S BRILLIANT BOOK FOR MORE ON AESTHETICS OF EXCESS THROUGH BLACK AND LATINX EMBODIMENT: "AESTHETICS

OF EXCESS ARE THE TARGETS OF COMMODIFICATION, APPROPRIATION, CULTURAL DISMISSAL, AND ERASURE—BUT THEY TEND TO SPECTACULARLY SURVIVE AND MORPH, SLIPPING THROUGH SUCH ATTEMPTS AT CAPTURE. IT'S HOW WE DRESS IN THE UNDERCOMMONS."

48 rhodes, *The Inheritance of Haunting*, 81.

49 R. Gutiérrez, *Brown Neon*.
SEE R. GUTIÉRREZ FOR MORE ON "BROWN NEON." THE CONCEPT OF BROWNNESS AS IT INTERFACES WITH TERRAIN AND INFRASTRUCTURE SHIFTS AND TRAVELS THROUGHOUT THE COLLECTION OF ESSAYS.

50 Muñoz, "The Brown Commons," in *The Sense of Brown*, 3.
SEE MUÑOZ FOR MORE ON BROWNNESS AS ARRIVAL.

51 Muñoz, *The Sense of Brown*, 2.
SEE MUÑOZ FOR MORE ON BROWNNESS AS CONTACT AND BEING ALONGSIDE.

52 Ramos, "Slow Encounters," 427.
IVÁN RAMOS REMINDS US THAT WE CAN'T ESCAPE THE "SOCIAL AND AFFECTIVE AFFINITIES" ACROSS AESTHETIC AND THEORETICAL SITES, OR WHAT HE CALLS "A QUEER TOUCH IN THE PRESENT" NEVER OUTSIDE OF BROWNNESS, BROWN SUBJECTS "WHO CONTINUOUSLY STAND OUTSIDE THE NORMATIVE DISCOURSE OF POLITICAL CHANGE, KEEPING THE IMMIGRANT IN A KIND OF IRRESOLVABLE TEMPORAL IMPASSE."

53 VOURLOUMIS, IN "TEN THESES ON TOUCH, OR, WRITING TOUCH," BEAUTIFULLY NOTES THE FOLLOWING: "THIS DISTRIBUTION OF THE SENSIBLE AND THE GAPS THEREIN EMERGE FROM DIFFERENT TIMES, SPACES, VOICES, POLITICS, AND AESTHETICS TOUCHING ME, TOUCHING YOU. TO BE TOUCHED BY AND TOUCH THESE PRACTICES, TEMPORALITIES, RESISTANCES IS, LIKE THE TOUCHING OF LANGUAGE, TO TOUCH ETERNAL OSCILLATION AND ALTERNATION: THE OSCULATION, MERGING, AND DISSOLUTION OF SUBJECT AND OBJECT."

54 Diaz, *Postcolonial Love Poem*.

55 Viego, *Dead Subjects*, 4.
I AM ALWAYS THINKING OF BROWNNESS ALONGSIDE ANTONIO VIEGO'S GENIUS *DEAD SUBJECTS*, IN WHICH TO BE BROWN ALREADY NECESSITATES A TYPE OF DEATH THAT INCLUDES THE POTENTIAL LIBERATION OF SUBJECTS IN THE PROSPECTS OF SUBJECT INCOMPLETION, OUTSIDE OF RACIALIZED TRANSPARENCIES.

56 Sharma, "Brown," 20.
SEE SHARMA FOR MORE ON HOW BROWNNESS, WHILE AN INCOMPLETE RACIAL FORMATION, STICKS AROUND.

57 Muñoz, *The Sense of Brown*, 2.
SEE MUÑOZ FOR MORE ON BROWNNESS AS "SWERVES OF MATTER."

58 ife, *Maroon Choreography*, ix.
SEE IFE FOR MORE ON ANACHOREOGRAPHY AND THE FERAL SPIRIT OF STUDY.

59　ife, *Maroon Choreography*, xi.
　　SEE IFE FOR MORE ON "STAMMERING," ENTANGLEMENT, AND "PNEUMATIC INTIMACIES."

60　ife, *Maroon Choreography*, xi.
　　SEE IFE FOR MORE ON THINGS OTHERWISE AND WISER CONFIGURATIONS.

61　Harney and Moten, *The Undercommons*, 30.
　　SEE HARNEY AND MOTEN FOR MORE ON HAPPENING IN HIDING.

62　J. M. Rodríguez, *Queer Latinidad*.
　　SEE JUANA MARÍA RODRÍGUEZ FOR MORE ON QUEER TRANSFORMATIONS OF LANGUAGE.

63　Sedgwick, "Queer and Now," 8.
　　Ahmed, "Conclusion," 208.
　　SEE SEDGWICK'S DEFINITION OF QUEER AS THE FOLLOWING: "THE OPEN MESH OF POSSIBILITIES, GAPS, OVERLAPS, DISSONANCES AND RESONANCES, LAPSES AND EXCESSES OF MEANING WHEN THEY CONSTITUENT ELEMENTS OF ANYONE'S GENDER, OF ANYONE'S SEXUALITY AREN'T MADE (OR *CAN'T* BE MADE) TO SIGNIFY MONOLITHICALLY." AND SEE AHMED'S IDEA THAT QUEER IS ABOUT HOW WE DELIBERATELY REFUSE "TO USE THINGS PROPERLY."

64　Iyer, "Exploding the Narrative in Jazz Improvisation," 394.
　　SEE IYER FOR MORE ON SUSTAINED ANTIPHONIES.

65　Ahmed, "Find Your Way," in *Queer Phenomenology*, 1.
　　SEE AHMED'S *QUEER PHENOMENOLOGY* FOR IDEAS ON ORIENTATION AND DISORIENTATION AS QUEER ONTOLOGICAL CHOREOGRAPHY.

66　Alvarado, "Ghostly Givings," 26.
　　SEE ALVARADO FOR MORE ON BROWNNESS AS HAUNTED COMMUNION.

67　Alvarado, *Abject Performances*.
　　Vargas, "Ruminations on Lo Sucio."
　　Beyoncé, "PURE/HONEY" and "Irreplaceable."

68　Noriega, "A Brown Study or a Usage Problem," 1.
　　SEE NORIEGA FOR MORE ON BROWN STUDY AND THE JUXTAPOSITION OF MELANCHOLY AND BROWN.

69　Noriega, "A Brown Study or a Usage Problem," 1.
　　SEE NORIEGA FOR MORE ON BROWN STUDY AS SOMETHING INTO WHICH A MAN IS LED.

70　Stein, "Golden Brown."
　　SEE STEIN FOR BROWN STUDY AND ITS USAGE IN THE SIXTEENTH CENTURY TO REFER TO INTENSE AND MELANCHOLY REVERIES.

71　Noriega, "A Brown Study or a Usage Problem," 2.
　　SEE NORIEGA FOR MORE ON BROWN STUDY AND BROWN AS A SPECTRUM OF COLORS AND A METAPHOR FOR RACIAL MIXTURE.

72 Guzmán, "Brown," 25.
    Muñoz, *Disidentifications*.
    Chambers-Letson, *After the Party*.
    Mudambi, "The Construction of Brownness."
    SEE THESE TEXTS FOR MORE ON HOW BROWN IS NOT A STABLE IDENTITY, BUT RATHER AN INCOHERENT AND INCOMMENSURABLE CATEGORY.

73 Stein, "Golden Brown."
    SEE STEIN FOR BROWN STUDY AND HOW THE TERM RESURFACES IN THE NINETEENTH CENTURY.

74 Guzmán, "Brown," 25.
    BROWNNESS, AS GUZMÁN REMINDS US, IS NEVER FULLY TRANSPARENT, EFFICIENT, "FULLY ENOUGH," OR DEVOID OF LOSS; IT EVOLVES IN LOSS AND "STAGES THE SMOLDERING INDENTION OF ITS OWN VULNERABILITY BY EXPOSING ITSELF TO ERASURE IN THE VERY ACT OF LONGING," A LONGING THAT NEVER STOPS EVOLVING, OR STUDYING (27).

75 Ramírez, *Colonial Phantoms*.
    SEE RAMÍREZ ON THE CONCEPT OF "GHOSTING": "'GHOSTING' IMPLIES THAT THE ACTS OF ERASURE THAT ARE PART AND PARCEL OF COLONIAL, IMPERIAL, AND MANY NATIONALIST PROJECTS HAVE PRODUCED NOT SO MUCH ACTUAL SILENCE AS OTHER UNWIELDY AND RECALCITRANT PRESENCES" (6).

76 Taylor, "Dancing with Diana."
    ACCORDING TO TAYLOR, REREADING DERRIDA'S THEORY OF HAUNTOLOGY, "THE GHOST IS BY DEFINITION A REPETITION, DERRIDA'S REVENANT" (64).

77 RESTREPO RHODES'S BEAUTIFUL BOOK CELEBRATES THE TRACES, LEGACIES, AND WORLDINGS OF OUR DEAD, MAKING CLEAR THAT GHOSTS AND SPIRITS REMAIN TO HELP PAVE OUR COLLECTIVE FUTURES.

78 Wright, *The Physics of Blackness*.
    THIS TEXT CAUTIONS US TO RECONSIDER THE POLEMICS OF RETURN IN THEIR CHAPTER "THE PROBLEM OF RETURN." WRIGHT STATES, "THE THOUGHT OF TRAVELING BACK THROUGH TIME IN A LINEAR PROGRESS NARRATIVE IS INHERENTLY LIMITED, BECAUSE PHYSICS SHOWS THAT OUR MOVEMENTS 'FORWARD' ARE ENTROPIC, NOT LINEAR" (76–77).

79 Rana, "Reading Brownness," 299.
    IN THIS ARTICLE, RANA STATES THAT READING BROWNNESS REQUIRES A REFORMULATION OF STUDY: "THIS IS A CHALLENGE THAT I PROPOSE 'BROWNNESS STUDIES' TAKE UP: TO UNDERSTAND BROWNNESS NOT JUST AS ANOTHER REHEARSAL OF POSTRACIAL IDEOLOGY BUT AS A PRODUCTIVE ENTROPY WITHIN IT, AS A COMPLEX NEW MANIFESTATION OF RACE AT THE PRESENT CONJUNCTURE" (299).

80 Ruiz, *Ricanness*, 136–39.

turn turn turn turn		turn turn turn turn
turn turn turn turn		turn turn turn turn
turn turn turn turn		turn turn turn turn
turn turn turn turn	turn	turn turn turn turn
turn turn turn turn		turn turn turn turn
turn turn turn turn		turn turn turn turn
turn turn turn turn		turn turn turn turn
turn turn turn turn		turn turn turn turn
turn turn turn turn		turn turn turn turn
turn turn turn turn		turn turn turn turn
turn turn turn turn	turn	turn turn turn turn
turn turn turn turn		turn turn turn turn
turn turn turn turn		turn turn turn turn
turn turn turn turn		turn turn turn turn
turn turn turn turn		turn turn turn turn
turn turn turn turn		turn turn turn turn
turn turn turn turn	turn	turn turn turn turn
turn turn turn turn		turn turn turn turn
turn turn turn turn		turn turn turn turn
turn turn turn turn		turn turn turn turn
turn turn turn turn		turn turn turn turn
turn turn turn turn		turn turn turn turn
turn turn turn turn	turn	turn turn turn turn
turn turn turn turn		turn turn turn turn
turn turn turn turn		turn turn turn turn
turn turn turn turn		turn turn turn turn
turn turn turn turn		turn turn turn turn
turn turn turn turn		turn turn turn turn
turn turn turn turn	turn	turn turn turn turn
turn turn turn turn		turn turn turn turn
turn turn turn turn		turn turn turn turn
turn turn turn turn		turn turn turn turn
turn turn turn turn		turn turn turn turn

IF WE WERE DEAD

would you read? Wet your beak
then plunge into expression
wielded by unsociable meter?

I only ask because my first love affair
was with a syllable—V's & C's opened then cinched
between immeasurable meaning. Long E's & magic vowels—
friendship-sounds. Any letter's utterance moved into idiom,
kin inner portals to the long horizon, eventual clause.

Resonance's silence—a drummer to time—
permanence's transience, a lightning phrase,
unending affections across rhythms accented.

Sometimes I've felt like the semicolon
joined to others in inseparable consent. Frequency
stresses & consonants intoned; noise-thoughts
drafted into couples, formed into a pause,
semi-full stop, together,

would you?

I only ask because every ghost is the ideal reader,
finding forever in interlude,
borrowed spaces & fissures, para-harmonies
in spirit topographies.

JUANGO & ROLAND

it's another weekend in lament pillages & gray boxes,
papercuts & papers stained, i find a black & white
photo tucked thoughtfully into forty-year-old plans—
bereft, subtly cracked, barely a belief, but she speaks,
susurrations, intense vibrational mmmmmms,
      hazy sound-hugs, history's long traveled airs.

i pull it from the folds

                                          slowly

fingers cold from concern,
creases liven, swivel & tell—
gossip's necessary archive.

i see her winter's garden,[1] a tiny stem about to grow,
snow petals in make-believe, sprung. split aesthetics
in frozen time. baby blankets to doleful boys, they hail.
she could never be their mother. never. but there's
ephemera again, heating up the absence of her gaze,
      filters lightly escape, the innocence of bare.

1   Barthes, *Camera Lucida*.

THIS POEM IS AN ENGAGEMENT WITH ROLAND BARTHES'S BOOK *CAMERA LUCIDA: REFLECTIONS ON PHOTOGRAPHY*—A BOOK SPLIT INTO TWO PARTS AND FORTY-EIGHT SMALL CHAPTERS. THE FIRST PART OF THE BOOK ENDEAVORS TO CREATE AN ONTOLOGY OF PHOTOGRAPHY THROUGH THE REINVENTION OF A VISUAL LEXICON. THE SECOND SECTION CONSISTS OF A SERIES OF GRIEF STILLS IN HOMAGE TO HIS BELATED MOTHER THROUGH AN IMAGE OF HER AS A CHILD, WHICH HE DESCRIBES BUT REFUSES TO SHARE WITH THE READER—*THE WINTER GARDEN PHOTO* (67).

FOLLOWING ARE A SERIES OF TURNS MADE WITH THE BOOK IN MEMORY OF IMAGES AND PARENTAL LOSS. THERE IS NO REAL TEMPORAL OR NUMERICAL ORDER TO MOURNING AND LOSS. IT IS OFTEN RANDOMLY SEEN AND FELT EVERYWHERE, AND SO THE LACK OF CHRONOLOGY HERE HOPES TO EXPRESS THAT TOO.

"There I was, alone in the apartment where she had died, looking at these pictures of my mother, one by one, under the lamp, gradually moving back in time with her, looking for the truth of the face I had loved. And I found it" (67).

"And here the essential question first appeared: did I recognize her?" (65).

"I had acknowledged that fatality, one of the most agonizing features of mourning, which decreed that however often I might consult such images, I could never recall her features (summon them up as a totality)" (63).

"She had become my little girl, uniting for me with that essential child she was in her first photograph" (72).

"Thus the life of someone whose existence has somewhat preceded our own encloses in its particularity the very tension of History, its division. History is hysterical: it is constituted only if we consider it, only if we look at it—and in order to look at it, we must be excluded from it" (64).

"... but the Winter Garden Photograph was indeed essential, it achieved for me, utopically, *the impossible science of the unique being*" (70–71).

"But my grief wanted a just image, an image which would be both justice and accuracy—*justesse*: just an image, but a just image. Such, for me, was the Winter Garden Photograph" (70).

"The almost: love's dreadful regime, but also the dream's disappointing status—which is why I hate dreams. For I often dream about her

(I dream only about her), but it is never quite my mother: sometimes, in the dream, there is something misplaced, something excessive: for example, something playful or casual—which she never was; or again I know it is she, but I do not see her features (but do we see, in dreams, or do we know?): I dream about her, I do not dream her" (66).

THE PAST OF AN IMAGE [1]

& this is how we parted.

        you, dimming bottom's crest

        eye, gazing glimmer's speed

        like a firefly to freedom's jar

        light fades genuinely sometimes

        flightless female, that could be me,

        & you, the fullest legacy of an·i·mat·ed debt

caught

      paid

           released

                  incurred

                        repeat

                              sold

    again. could you not press against ambition's spirit?
inherited restlessness never rescues

    the surface. & we knew that.
    we always knew that.

     gleaming relic
   holding so tightly
     to the deadest ringer
  of the deadest effigy
   to hold

off

finger's loosening grip—
because spillages rumor nothing

      about being our being

settler affinities in (de)montage, reverse, sped up,
rewound frames—lightless stills upon stills &

   you,
   brown girl,
   could be everyone's illusion

     in climbing
     you tighten *that* lid
     freeze sight
     & end wing's fire

---

1 Rancière, *The Future of the Image*.
   THIS POEM'S TITLE IS A RIFF ON JACQUES RANCIÈRE'S 2007 BOOK TITLE *THE FUTURE OF THE IMAGE*.

SPLITTING AIR

Defeated by consequence
    & forced
to hold my breath

would you return
    to *terra indígena*
& be my sigh?

I'll wait for us
    in the inhale
respiration is a two-

spirit exhale
    lessons in melody
lent by themes.

WHERE THE TIMID TAKE THEIR NOSES FOR A WALK

they skim every syllable from handbooks
intentional confidence & care
paragraphically timed ethics & impending hisses

this future
   that future
      post-futures
no future

trainings & scenarios
people of color, color-to-the-people, performing power
to truth, clip-on ties, polyester suits &
I just sold my soul for a retention

contracts surrender owners
long-winded chains, gurgling please & *I just want my mom*

temper
temper
temper

the ear to institutional tantrums turned traumas
everything they spew—a line to lay you down to deaf

like protest songs to gas
like protest gas to arms

in reminder, we little remain
in reminder, we little remain

MIS C A R R I E D

I look for the beginning in blue

& listen for dead yellow.

White lights, watery greens, clay bones,

I see form above meaning.

Timbre to echoes & valve-less hearts,
          I pretend each loss is red

catching up to brown
          at the dawn of gray.

Lavender graves with no-name plots

     where feral cats squat & piss.

There's black at center stage, main squeeze

          of pass & play.

Color monuments & cloudless tears,

exit wounds[1] & muted applause—such imperfect fissures

          indigo & violet.

1   Vuong, *Night Sky with Exit Wounds*.

TURNTURNTURNTURNTURNTURNTURNTURNTURNTURNTURNTURNTURNTURNTURN
TURNTURNTURNTURNTURNTURNTURNTURNTURNTURNTURNTURNTURNTURNTURN
TURNTURNTURNTURNTURNTURNTURNTURNTURNTURNTURNTURNTURNTURNTURN
TURNTURNTURNTURNTURNTURNTURNTURNTURNTURNTURNTURNTURNTURNTURN
TURNTURNTURNTURNTURNTURNTURNTURNTURNTURNTURNTURNTURNTURNTURN
TURNTURNTURNTURNTURNTURNTURNTURNTURNTURNTURNTURNTURNTURNTURN
TURNTURNTURNTURNTURNTURNTURNTURNTURNTURNTURNTURNTURNTURNTURN

FOR THE PEOPLE FROM THE STARS

We could be stranded between something's splattered dust & the paradox of planetary promise, midday forgotten, twice risen by earth, many times removed

>	like black holes
>	to baby stars
>	in dwarf galaxies.

I remember this remembrance as a courtesy to belong. Listen for threshold grunts, able groans in able aphorisms:

>	cite the furiously hushed, indelicately prodded,
>	cultivated against, the those & them, speech
>	acts & *tildes*, foremothers of no singular
>	land, all property & worth.

We could become those eclipses showering light across the sky, squelching tiny into disappearing acts. We could feel the moon's shadow like the last tingle of the first homage, borrowing from sketches of anything's after, vibrant smudges & endnotes

>	collective blurs
>		fades to black
>			astral happenings

fall

        fall

                fall

                        fall

i

                                  n

                                                            g

there could be a way

INNER-CITY JUICE BOXES

If we were still best friends
we'd sit on the front stoop,
our fingers laced,
juice boxes in liberated hands.

I'd be pigeon-toed,
your heels would touch,
we'd name stars,
make faces at the clouds.

Slurping into space
like traveling time scenes
with every gulp, we'd pause.

I'd say, *pa, can the stars see us?*
You'd say, *if we scream loud enough, mija.*

Following your lead,
we'd begin to feel each giggle,
from our bellies into the blue
like well-off echoes brimming streets.

You'd say, *did the clouds hear us?*
I'd say, *only if we close our eyes, papi.*

Turning to the sky & then to one another
we'd shrink in our chins. With blushed
cheeks, sight silences & empty cartons—

we'd be each other's dreams.

BLEMISH *(TITLED TWICE)*

to be a butterfly on your back you will never feel

a movement piece in stillness for senseless skin

to listen for refrains wane breathlessness

                                            arrest patience

                  refuse flutter

                            all wings

                                              just a shiver of another day

ACADEMIA DESCENDED: EMANCIPATORY LOVE WORDS

I'd walk down the aisle
if I could leave in the morning.

                                                I'd give you
                                               something
                                                  if you'd
                                               never ask
                                            for everything.

I'd change light bulbs, fix pipes, collect
trash if you'd forget me when I yield.

                                          I'd bake bread,
                                              fry bacon,
                                           clean sheets,
                                   sweep bathroom hair
                            if you'd never refuse to share.

                  I'd say three little words,
             plant seeds in embryo gardens,
             make smiles of Tuesday frowns
          if only you'd leave the back door open.

AHA! IN FRAGMENTS

when the sky breaks open
inhale her whisper.

she holds hushed aces for the living.

gravid stones for lungs,
rock-solid burdens & genetic pipe dreams,

she tames calamity
into depths of friendship.

sermon lessons in cosmic study

three parts affable winds
four parts courteous forgiveness,

she trims terror's obesity.

READING DEBTS

haunted by an image
that is really a sound
feeling travels
at the intersection
of phonetics & touch

the cast of a sentence—not mine, not yours, but theirs

a body's metric
mimetic
mimic
mine

to be theirs. to be theirs.
to not be there, but here
as theirs.
raped by the border logics of rhythm.
theirs. to be theirs.

to whom does the sound belong?
theirs.

to never dot their eyes, cross their teas,
make the number ate into infinity signs like eight.

to be theirs.
be not
there,
but theirs.

if they had a paragraph
for every person
they couldn't read
would everyone become a chapter
they couldn't finish?

to be theirs. to be there. in the temporal
register of forever
unturned

to be theirs. to be theirs. to be theirs.
not to be there,
but here
as
theirs.

turn turn turn turn turn turn turn turn turn turn turn turn
turn turn turn turn turn turn turn turn turn turn turn turn
turn turn turn turn turn turn turn turn turn turn turn turn
turn turn turn turn turn turn turn turn turn turn turn turn
turn turn turn turn turn turn turn turn turn turn turn turn
turn turn turn turn turn turn turn turn turn turn turn turn
turn turn turn turn turn turn turn turn turn turn turn
turn turn turn turn turn turn turn turn turn turn
turn turn turn turn turn turn turn turn turn
turn turn turn turn turn turn turn turn
turn turn turn turn turn turn turn
turn turn turn turn turn turn
turn turn turn turn turn turn turn turn turn turn
turn turn turn turn turn turn turn turn turn turn turn
turn turn turn turn turn turn turn turn turn turn turn turn
turn turn turn turn turn turn turn turn turn turn turn turn
turn turn turn turn turn turn turn turn turn turn turn turn
turn turn turn turn turn turn turn turn turn turn turn turn
turn turn turn turn turn turn turn turn turn turn turn turn
turn turn turn turn turn turn turn turn turn turn turn turn
turn turn turn turn turn turn turn turn turn turn turn turn
turn turn turn turn turn turn turn turn turn turn turn turn
turn turn turn turn turn turn turn turn turn turn turn
turn turn turn turn turn turn turn turn turn turn turn
turn turn turn turn turn turn turn turn turn turn turn
turn turn turn turn turn turn turn turn turn turn turn
turn turn turn turn turn turn turn turn turn turn turn
turn turn turn turn turn turn turn turn turn turn
turn turn turn turn turn turn turn turn turn
turn turn turn turn turn turn turn turn
turn turn turn turn turn turn turn turn turn
turn turn turn turn turn turn turn turn turn turn

TO BE SOFT

We will spit out our tongues[1] and watch them walk—soldiering toward the sea *en masse*, en three. Tippy-toe struts, intangible wings & pearl sweats in ripple sway.

There will be diligent flow from one phrase to a million screams, upside-down triangles faithful to the drift like water weapons, no teeth for grout. Gravity's foe.

Eventually the sky will drink. Bloated soft. Communal echoes without cheeks. Monologues turned chorus forward in replay, mutinous clouds soaring in utterance.

To be soft, to be soft, to be soft, to be soft: underground activities in celestial pellets, to be soft, to be soft, to be soft, to be soft, to be soft, to soft *be*.

---

1   Anzaldúa, *Borderlands / La Frontera*.
Riggs, *Tongues United*.
THIS POEM SAT WITH THESE TWO OBJECTS IN ORDER TO SOFTEN THE WORDS THAT EXTEND FROM THE TONGUE.

NECROPOLITICAL   FEMINISM

I loved the institution like well to water. Elongated
pulls, pauses & do-overs in displeasure & thirst. Golden

cuffs & spittle showers, hand-me-down managers & casual
chokeholds, senile leather whips & turn-page paper cuts.

        Everyone just a little damp.

                                    Everything just a little stolen.

                              Tender throats along the swallow
                                  citing politics like queers
                                            to forgetting.

LET'S TOUCH

where do we sit when no one is left standing?
                             just a bunch of sad Brown girls[1]
                             shrinking with the moon

communal pinky-swears to feel lonely together
                         until crescent's peak tears
                         un/patchable holes
                         through the wall

     a resting spot

     light wind
     aphonic apologies

                             tiny fingers on the other side

---

[1] FOR ALL THE WOMEN-OF-COLOR FEMINISTS AND QUEER WOMEN OF COLOR AND QUEER AND TRANS WOMEN HERE NOW IN THIS PLANE AND IN MY EVERYDAY, I OFFER TOUCH FROM THE OTHER SIDE. MAY WE NEVER FORGET TO HOLD ONE ANOTHER IN DEEPEST RESPECT AND SPIRITUAL PLENITUDE; THERE'S ENOUGH FOR ALL OF US; WE ARE ENOUGH. WITH A FINGER'S TOUCH AND LOVE TO SLK, APR, M.LC, PVC, RNB, HV, LC, IM, LMC, BRE, NR, BES, CO, MC, IH, EG, AK, AG, ZG, AS, LA, EF, BR, MPR, AV, KB, MA, YR, SS, NR, RG, LA, JH, SP, JD, GG. LET THE INITIAL BECOME ANOTHER INVITATION.

INCOMPLETION AS VERSE

the second act of study is withdrawal—

a repressed sneeze in winter
cold enough to unhear
but frozen into the free

key pitches in unremitting tunes.

icicled compositions in cunning parts
parts to the cunning compositions: icicled.

to trust this sound is to commit to the violence of a sentence.

KIMCHI & TACOS

Deep strums
begging for teardrops

tender hits in tender's raw
ingested lyrics pass on

feelings are feeling this, recipes—
nostalgic
entombed

imbibing the downbeat
to catch sway

Enters the narrator:

Whenever she sees people of color cook together, she remembers crunch silences & grease sparks awakening the dead into renewed mourning. Like songs in eccentric melody—Koreans speaking Spanish, Latinas voicing Swahili over hotbeds of coconut rice, red beans, roasted pork & pentatonic black keys. ~~Memory scales from this taste to a million auras; in a pinch, everything lost is suddenly scored.~~

I GUESS I FORGIVE YOU

directions: read without pause; every sound is a space for them.

what if love were how we did study together in the roaming halls of future learning losing time like thinkers in chambers of dimensional stop signs where they find tick tock dancing in sync too othered why did it sound like empty verbs losing single guitar strums communal chords semi-broken semi-alive where we watch dog shit & ideologies merge shrewd slates of plural seeing where the lonely benches meet mating birds & we all wonder where's the seat cushion to the revolutionary armchairs did no one win after throwing rocks at sisters like bullets into dehydrated ponds with bomb lines & liquid shores leaking into our tongues we could be laboring comrades reciting hymns for battle in june no tombs for long lives & ancestors are all her now them us what if study were

                                                                                enough

turn turn turn turn turn turn turn turn turn turn turn turn turn turn turn turn turn turn turn turn turn turn turn turn

TITLED TWICE (*BLEMISH*)

Could we wander past our flesh
& squeeze the haze inside? Stroll-

skip & fly-float to courage's
pulse, pocket-sized shifts

& dusky footprints, the hoary
broken syncopate, reviving

time's riff. Past pose & swagger,
looking glasses sonically quiver

for those forever lost. Internal
grounds croon, gyrate, shimmy-lift

the lonesome, bathing dry
to dress up the heart's respite.

LAS   **ELOISAS**

our world is a sea upside down
to be under her is to skip
on sodden clouds

                               aaaaaaah, if we were all birds . . .

hope's flight
no jet dares glide

                                     murder allies caw
                                     glistening kin

circling

           circling

                     circling

                                     wings descend—
                                         suspire like lungs

landing friendships

                               fly

                                             again

WITH JUAN GABRIEL Y CAMILA

(for s.g.)

To keep her name today—

        it's February: the month she was born

on a day near the evening she passed.

        Unborn boys & unfinished girls

surviving bitter burials of birth.

Such trouble to speak in the pros & cons of nouns. They say. They say. It's easy to think in silhouettes, dress parts, be mindful of mothers

        with toes fixed on fathering frontiers.

        Binaries like arsenal
        who is whoever to whomever
        us-they

crossings in swans & sailors,
dry land meets water meets vacant wombs,

        still travels & wayward currents.

He's in every shadow, a queen fit for a queen—
Juan Gabriel, he whispers: you're still here, Camila?

She'll be everything otherwise answered.

    Blue-femme

                fragrance   form

    contoured obscurity

beyond reticence & conviction

                you couldn't leave?

LONELINESS PROPERTY

have you ever folded a white sheet of paper in half
only to have it flap open like a champagne socialist
during combat? you lick your thumbnail, wet the spine,
top to end, in eminent closure, but the moisture
splits. two sides of left.

once a point plan
now slippery sets
def(r)amed portraits

in neon dashikis, rainbow berets & brown lavender

through the mouth of buck trickery
on the plates of privation
behind the eye of binding form
off come the pos(t)ers & people
like interruptions in looping time

FOG PLAY

I'll be the endurance to your sprint

bring you back inelegantly

noontimes' escapade, save lunch,

a little after the quarter moon

half-life right behind my teeth

like desperation

to yesterday's unsociable tomorrow,

the alarm will shake.

SUDDENLY A SENSE

                to sound like a wound in a whisper
                divergent scream
                humbled purr
                the arrogant hiss
                felt in treble graze
                ambitious silence
                attuned affliction
                incommunicative flashbacks blaring
                if only the flesh would flake
                swig its residue
                be a little more than a murmur

to hear an injury
wearing the casket's creak—
corporeality
              made verse

                        shouldering innuendos

                        lulls-limbs-loss

a violin's split string

a violin's split string

turn & turn &

BROWN BOYS

I only remember us
when sunlight & dew
steal steam-beams
& shadow-shapes
into fainting window-
panes. Wind pain.

Shoulders collapse
like arches of debt: filmy outlines—
wistful erasures made trace,
traced erased.

There's no spark in our pit.
Unexcited burnouts, exit flames,
left edges: lip-lined contempt.

Specters of capital—
afterlives gasping
through frenzies of industry.

Thirsty graves & unhungry tombs,
shoreless water's fall,
empty tillage &
another
fatherless
Monday.

Loyal worry & rebellious sorrow
make grief-play make labor-late,
so I squeeze burnt skin
into the breaks of our mama's

mama's fork—too thick to stay
inside the lines until I can,

I can,
I can,
I can.

Egg drips & coffee drops
catch shirts, meet the lonely.
Not the silk texture
of expensive suffering—
but the pedestrian
button-down
unbuttoned-buttoned.

Every morning bites like this:
combustible raven squares
sucking air out of senile skies.
Flinging forgiveness into night

meanders, camera-eye affections—
loss, loss, lost over empty
cups & crushed silences.

FOUND IN UNDERTONE

there's a compass tied to her belt
but she never looks down

skyscrapers are like girls to her

pining to climb & slide over. instead, fleece
hats & tweed gloves, overworn & borrowed

edging gently

near enough

hesitantly

textile innuendos

drifting across a winter's sigh.

bitsy vexed ambitions to uncrowned desires
she stares above the psychic fray,
militant heights, '60s-colonial-shine,
she whisper walks.

    underground feelings rove west
          aerial thoughts steer east

city metronome sympathies
sync-stirring
in femme transport,
she walks.

she walks
knowing hand silence
is the only way to quiet touch
taller than towers,
taller than her.

FRIENDLESS

                                        The pandemic made us friendless.

Everyone we love is dead. Everyone alive hates living.
To hold, to let go, to say *I miss you* over a dropped call,
the feedback—

                                                  I'm sorry.

Underwater testimonies in ground-level receipts: *I hope t-*
/\/\/\/\/\/*new*/\/\/\/\/\/*it's*\/\/\/\/\/\/\/\/\/\/\/\/\/\/
\/\/\/\/\/\/\/\/\/\/\/\/\/\/\/\/\/*been*\/\/\/\/\/\/\/\/
/\/\/\/\/\/*since*/\/\/\/\/\/..
....
....
....
....
....
....

slivered names, stretched

                                                                      e
                                                                      a
                                                                      r
                                                                      s

                            are we still (t)here?

OOOOOOOOOOOOOOO

Not a philosopher
Not a philosopher
Knot a philosopher
Knot a philosopher
Entangled by the premise
Not knotted in praxis.

AA: ACADEMIA ASCENDED

If I told you I could see the future would you believe me?

misty film stills
shot-reverse-shots
overlays & laps
time beams, faded pinks

salted folds, blurs
& aerial growls

OR

gentle ambushes
clutching tongues
left
(of center)
out breathing the wind

unrequited humility—

                wolves

                        chained to anti-communal chairs

immeasurable

              longing

      &

disquieting
gratitude

LA LUZ NOT MINE

> We hold tragedy
> like unsinkable brigades
> pinching away sustenance
> & memory & closeness & fear—
> those other, other names
> for *dressage*'s love
> weighing heavily
> like animus to lightning.
>
> Charring emergencies,
> we will hardly remember,
>
> bodies unturned return
> still to drill borrowed land
> & mind-wave furiously
> to the sea's bottom.
>
> Such depthless
> inefficiencies
> to brush freedom. Big

space

between hailstorms & war showers.

turn	turn	turn	turn	turn	turn	turn	turn	turn
turn	turn	turn	turn	turn	turn	turn	turn	turn
turn	turn	turn	turn	turn	turn	turn	turn	turn
turn	turn	turn	turn	turn	turn	turn	turn	turn
turn	turn	turn	turn	turn	turn	turn	turn	turn
turn	turn	turn	turn	turn	turn	turn	turn	turn
turn	turn	turn	turn	turn	turn	turn	turn	turn
turn	turn	turn	turn	turn	turn	turn	turn	turn
turn	turn	turn	turn	turn	turn	turn	turn	turn
turn	turn	turn	turn	turn	turn	turn	turn	turn
turn	turn	turn	turn	turn	turn	turn	turn	turn
turn	turn	turn	turn	turn	turn	turn	turn	turn
turn	turn	turn	turn	turn	turn	turn	turn	turn
turn	turn	turn	turn	turn	turn	turn	turn	turn
turn	turn	turn	turn	turn	turn	turn	turn	turn
turn	turn	turn	turn	turn	turn	turn	turn	turn
turn	turn	turn	turn	turn	turn	turn	turn	turn
turn	turn	turn	turn	turn	turn	turn	turn	turn
turn	turn	turn	turn	turn	turn	turn	turn	turn
turn	turn	turn	turn	turn	turn	turn	turn	turn
turn	turn	turn	turn	turn	turn	turn	turn	turn
turn	turn	turn	turn	turn	turn	turn	turn	turn
turn	turn	turn	turn	turn	turn	turn	turn	turn
turn	turn	turn	turn	turn	turn	turn	turn	turn
turn	turn	turn	turn	turn	turn	turn	turn	turn
turn	turn	turn	turn	turn	turn	turn	turn	turn
turn	turn	turn	turn	turn	turn	turn	turn	turn
turn	turn	turn	turn	turn	turn	turn	turn	turn

WATCHING DREAMS *CON* LORD LYDIA

There's this queer[1] girl
crushed by fading stars.
She bargains with melancholy
in an act of cruel optimism.[2]

The galaxy dims her light. The moon shadows her sun.

She says:

        I'll never forget myself as a ten-year-old
        looking out the back-seat window of a dark
        red station wagon, at the cornfields, cows,
        & wide horizon, crying my eyes because
        eventually the solar system would die
        & all of it would be gone without a trace.

She gathers her shame to sleep against sonorous desire.

Lord Lydia: taken before any counted sheep.

---

1   *A veces la llamamos cuir y al escuchar, nos encontramos.*
     FOR JULIA, WHO FEELS THE SKY AND LISTENS FOR SHAPES.

2   Berlant, *Cruel Optimism*.
     TO INVOKE LAUREN BERLANT'S 2011 *CRUEL OPTIMISM* IS TO GENTLY TURN
     TO THEM—INSUFFICIENTLY, OF COURSE, LIKE ALL THE DELIBERATE WAYS ONE
     LOOKS TO THE STARS TO RETURN A SENSE OF JUSTICE TO LOSS.

TAINTED LIVE WITH A DESK

If the first act of love is study
to extol its virtue
we must unlearn

everything.

SCORE FOR THE SAND

sunless brows dip, dip,
dive like novice swimmers
uncovering the shallows
where water bans break

lashes clump & furrows curl
weighted valleys wounded,
fate streams & teardrop pellets—
shape-textures for this world's
marching thresh-holds.

there's death in our vision—
laid-up yellow & slippery red,
scratched light, coffee gusted gawks
& right turn speckles tugged,
passive force, gaped pasts.

there are no laps left. blink. the earth
knows when to sit & wait. the desert,
sightless, spites its site &

        now we wear eye-shields
        toward History & gaze
        tomorrow for the undrowned.[1]

---

1   Gumbs, *Undrowned.*
     THINKING WITH ALEXIS PAULINE GUMBS'S *UNDROWNED: BLACK FEMINIST LESSONS FROM MARINE MAMMALS* AND *M ARCHIVE: AFTER THE END OF THE WORLD.*

I REMEMBER US TALKING ABOUT LACAN THROUGH J

It was navy black into the light, cold enough to feel
your toes from the distance. The fire crossed flames
into monologues, there like that, a memory whisked
like that, there. You gazed across the pit like a curious
mourner fawning infinite desire. There, like that, there.
Into the empty with floating fog swirls & clarities of
promise, straddling stations & searching redemptions.
There. Like that. We live on through the other, to the
other side, the formless. Like that.

*Whenever I hear the word love I always think of J citing
Lacan. Love is that thing that you don't WANT to give
to someone who doesn't want it. Sorry, sorry, so sorry,
I really meant that love is that thing that you don't HAVE
that you want to give to someone who doesn't want it.*

The stillness of sentiment masks the silly gesture
into grief-odes, another word for care felt like a comet
drowning in underbelly (gracefully explosive!), & even
if no one wants it, you offer it up like decade-stained pennies
to a wishing well. Love, you say, love you don't have &
love they don't want? How vastly broken language's thirst
in excess swallow, the present forever not in ever-presence?
How do we speak for the shapeless?

*It's like lifting old candy from the bodega: the cereal-colored cat
watching; the major excitement, peeling off the wrapper &
Lacan's high tempered meow. Eventually everything disappears
& we meet again in reproduction's fade.*

ANYBODY'S ANYBODY

I found her like road rage
to remains. A social wound
painted in lazy avenues.

Dressed for missing-mass-tea
& post-Saturday rum bumps,
la dona sin ñ, historically bare.

Pale pink *bata,* layered lint
pimples & *manteca* stains,
cream slippers turned pecan,

government frames taped twice,
burnt tips & wet dentures, too many
texture-smells to say her name.

                                        anybody's anybody,
                                    anybody's
                                              anybody,

                                  anybody's
                                        anybody,

                         any-
                            body

Unsought soil to stricken seeds
or an overused napkin
coiled into loneliness?

She's a whistling radiator (9th floor),
kitchen curtains dirty of espionage,
speaking-in-tongue cabinets,

four-day-old decaf coffee
sin sugar cubes *y pan tostao*
edged in mold

                                        anybody's anybody, anybody's
                                               mother (of color), a shot

                              from a discount movie
                                        rewound to fast-forward,

                                      she's a visual hush.

                anybody's
                          anybody
                                    anybody's

                        any

                                      body

THE EARLESS SHARK OR STILL A JANITOR'S KID

I spend the first of May waiting for signifiers to rewire skylines into nonfiction rallies. Cosmic compositions. Major key. The striking elbows endure the secret's refrain. There's this fiery itch, an auditory laceration in my right ear. It drowns space into background sight for political bands without names.

I ask the left: is this the end of listening? A buzzing crawl into the poli-musical—a tiny bit goth, in-sync bass funk, jazz salsas, sax non-solo disco drops, hype-queers, and freestyle rebounds. Improvised ensembles in co-presence kinetics, working people blues, willful cha-chas & movement making mutiny; scores as world as wild is west.

    I scratch it.

                                                     I scratch it.

From one turning table
to records bound-inbound
enters vibration & voice
like swerve to sway
bounce to house

                                                    we scratch.
                                   we scratch it.

(turn) (turn) (turn) (turn) (turn) (turn) (turn) (turn) (turn) (turn)
(turn) (turn) (turn) (turn) (turn) (turn) (turn) (turn) (turn) (turn)
(turn) (turn) (turn) (turn) (turn) (turn) (turn) (turn) (turn) (turn)
(turn) (turn) (turn) (turn) (turn) (turn) (turn) (turn) (turn) (turn)
(turn) (turn) (turn) (turn) (turn) (turn) (turn) (turn) (turn) (turn)
(turn) (turn) (turn) (turn) (turn) (turn) (turn) (turn) (turn) (turn)
(turn) (turn) (turn) (turn) (turn) (turn) (turn) (turn) (turn) (turn)
(turn) (turn) (turn) (turn) (turn) (turn) (turn) (turn) (turn) (turn)
(turn) (turn) (turn) (turn) (turn) (turn) (turn) (turn) (turn) (turn)
(turn) (turn) (turn) (turn) (turn) (turn) (turn) (turn) (turn) (turn)
(turn) (turn) (turn) (turn) (turn) (turn) (turn) (turn) (turn) (turn)
(turn) (turn) (turn) (turn) (turn) (turn) (turn) (turn) (turn) (turn)
(turn) (turn) (turn) (turn) (turn) (turn) (turn) (turn) (turn) (turn)
(turn) (turn) (turn) (turn) (turn) (turn) (turn) (turn) (turn) (turn)
(turn) (turn) (turn) (turn) (turn) (turn) (turn) (turn) (turn) (turn)
(turn) (turn) (turn) (turn) (turn) (turn) (turn) (turn) (turn) (turn)
(turn) (turn) (turn) (turn) (turn) (turn) (turn) (turn) (turn) (turn)
(turn) (turn) (turn) (turn) (turn) (turn) (turn) (turn) (turn) (turn)
(turn) (turn) (turn) (turn) (turn) (turn) (turn) (turn) (turn) (turn)
(turn) (turn) (turn) (turn) (turn) (turn) (turn) (turn) (turn) (turn)
(turn) (turn) (turn) (turn) (turn) (turn) (turn) (turn) (turn) (turn)
(turn) (turn) (turn) (turn) (turn) (turn) (turn) (turn) (turn) (turn)
(turn) (turn) (turn) (turn) (turn) (turn) (turn) (turn) (turn) (turn)
(turn) (turn) (turn) (turn) (turn) (turn) (turn) (turn) (turn) (turn)
(turn) (turn) (turn) (turn) (turn) (turn) (turn) (turn) (turn) (turn)
(turn) (turn) (turn) (turn) (turn) (turn) (turn) (turn) (turn) (turn)
(turn) (turn) (turn) (turn) (turn) (turn) (turn) (turn) (turn) (turn)
(turn) (turn) (turn) (turn) (turn) (turn) (turn) (turn) (turn) (turn)
(turn) (turn) (turn) (turn) (turn) (turn) (turn) (turn) (turn) (turn)
(turn) (turn) (turn) (turn) (turn) (turn) (turn) (turn) (turn) (turn)

DECEMBER'S THIRD: THE ENDNOTE

"No one writes death like I do"—I say to myself
on a train, through the park, into stores & schools
& others who memory-lane me with funeral
stories of widows jumping into caskets &
overestimating reverends overeating rice pudding
over small talk with mono-emotional mothers.

It's another anniversary & I feel forgotten
by forgetting; everything's an endnote,
a little unwritten. I do the things one does
in non-aftermaths of grief (*palabritas tan dulce*)
only to ask for every syllable back—
"how could you know loss like me?" It's a question
this time, unspoken & unanswered, but it
penetrates basalt (my heart, an unbodying grunt).
I shed stubborn tears, forever falling
while stories persist (ghost visions, *velas
prendidas*, spirit numbers & always fainting *tías*).

I don't know if everyone else knows dying
like they know bodies, or if sharing warm drinks
makes us future death-friends, but I pull out
a poem from spades of brown sorrow (something
about loss being the paradox of love) & I spit out
a verse: "grief is where lungs become one."

This time my eyes giggle
& I fear quietly like it happened to Yesterday—
"do you *now* know you're a citation?"

FLAWED I'M POSSIBLE TOO OR FLAWED IMPOSSIBLE TO

There's something ominous in the number 2—

the sometimes swirl, knotted shape, squiggly boneless elbows rolled into stops,

2.

I find half a heart in it, a swan bending lines & massacred secrets,

2.

THE FUTURE OF THE FUTURE

(primas)[1]

if we must feel anything in what unfeeling opens,
glove the pavement's heartbeat. syncopation is a life
& every finger, the same question: was the violence

from us,

                                                                   or for us?

once, we wore revolutionary teeth as colonial fists
or was it imperial tongues to insurgency's lisp?

      played psych games for chess pawns
      talked-the-talk in cheap chicago jaunts
      look alike sisters skillful in soul beatdowns

           none of them double-
           dutched, ran through
           thunderous hydrants,
           beaded braids & returned
           secondhand hoops

           none of them rage danced
           battles to rainless block

parties

      because none of them wet/wept with hip-hop

verses dried to dripple
& in the space between alley fights & hunger pains
& peeping toms & grannies watching

we wrote

& our streets were ripple sounds again

---

1   I'VE BEEN THINKING A LOT ABOUT INNER-CITY ACTS OF FAMILY FORMATION THAT COME FROM FORMLESS GENEALOGIES. OR THE WAYS IN WHICH WE RENAME FOLKS—PET NAMES, NICKNAMES, SOMETIMES FALSE NAMES, UGLY NAMES, FUN NAMES, AND THEN SHARE OUR FAMILY NAMES—AND HOW THAT RENAMING PROVIDES A TURN TO NEW FORMS OF KINSHIP AS STUDY.

EPHEMERALITY'S BREEZE

I fly over your signature with my index finger
                                                seven loyal years

down, up, over a loop, into shadowgraphs,
typographies, common slopes
sleepy letters & lovebird diphthongs

missed mementos silently sung
auto attentive do-it-again
                again
          again

spirals, sinuous humps
dots, snake waves

line-bonds

our breath   between letters

                              absentia

                                        in open

                  drift
                        touch
                  drift
                       touch

                                        suddenly an us

EPILOGUES & CIRCLES

Tobacco

                                                                                 curled

willfully   into a soliloquy

                                         hand rehearsals for looking away

a good-bye breakfast

                                                        wanton-what-was

                    lips

to unsweetened coffee

phantom brushes against the collar

                                              land

predictable catchups

whole milk & silver spoons
not room temperature

                                                          legacies

New Yorkers flicker by   severed   waltzes
back   bends &   toe presses
shoulders up. chin   ahead as
                                            puffs
become passes

              nomadic street scenes in quotidian repeat

burning smirks & stale drafts

                    waiters gone waitress

rescued by

                                break

              d(a/o)wn

        I always thought closure happened
     over night-sky dinners: synonymous pasts,
      you & I, like double-dipped finger-licked
     plantain chips & overserved lemon drops,
        we'd be dead full of one another.

ALTAR GIRLS *EN FAJARDO*

she never said her name—anonymous, alone, alive: ocean.

imagine ice fishing *en fajardo*

impossible jumbo perch & walleyes

anticipating hooks, casting nets

like stench to commitment

spoiled shacks & soiled voyages

operations in boots & straps

cross-water buzz & relic bubbles

unreliable rafts & plane lifts

mortal commerce & colonial collegiality

      spaces between that & near,
      no more tangible than far to here,
      where the only bait caught
      is the wealth uncommon to the commons.

anonymous, alive, alone: ocean—she never said her name.

the gut's pebble now a future-us strewn along the bank.

END WITH BIRDS
(*ONCE WE ALL FLEW*)

I hope that Hitchcock movie[1] comes alive & birds recover the world, he says, believing in films to rescue us whole. He stares at the clouds (woolly upbeat splendors) & I wonder, like light to blind, has he been saved by the flock, or is he just willing to die, unlike the rest of us who sit bi, to watch by, bye-bye, escaping seething cascades?

Wouldn't you like to witness a million black birds, lovesick by chaotic makeover, repairing tricks-to-treats into new world orders? Poke-rubs to one percent pupils, or pecking dots to wet cheeks?

I wouldn't.

I, like anger to uninvited graves, look down,

               down,
               down,
               down

               &

         down into tunnels' bottom's
         underground's lapses.

Ancestors underneath, itchy with sleep, begin to shake deliberately. Contented waiting they call it—

             ready

           to

            soar

              again?

---

1 Hitchcock, *The Birds*.

UNBODYING GRUNT

She can't remember all of you, just the hushed pricks
    turned water wrinkles for blue light homecomings
& yet she'd drown again to brush you at the bottom.
Close-ups in weighted histories & sermon sighs, she'll
    be host for ground's le prime; not an unreliable body
in D minor—those left-hand finger keystrokes welcoming
    solemnity's sounding—but symphonies
    gone muted-aloof   tuned[1]

---

[1] THIS POEM ORIGINALLY APPEARED IN "ATLAS: SKIN/BONE/BLOOD: BODY MAPS IN BROWN AND BLACK," *APOGEE JOURNAL* 18 (OCTOBER 2022), A SPECIAL POETRY ISSUE ON LATINX DISABILITIES. WITH SPECIAL THANKS TO MY FELLOW BRILLIANT CONTRIBUTORS, ALONG WITH EDITORS JOEY DE JESUS, ZEYFR LISOWSKI, AND HEIDI ANDREA RESTREPO RHODES.

BASQUIAT'S RIDE

to be[1]

    an envelope after the letter's read
    a Brooklyn street bed colored restless

    a tiny sullen ghost rewrapped in dust,
    riding airwave ideas. (im)material

    slivers of something once left
    unturned, drifting spirit first

                                      into infinitude.

    an almost brushstroke at concept's edge
    almost masterpiece, seeing between scene.

    an image opens, water drowns.
    yesterday's canvas—painted weightless.

---

[1] Basquiat, *Riding with Death*.
Moten, "jean-michel basquiat," 21.
THIS POEM SAT WITH TWO ARTIFACTS: BASQUIAT'S 1988 PAINTING *RIDING WITH DEATH* AND FRED MOTEN'S POEM "JEAN-MICHEL BASQUIAT"—A SITTING THAT SWIVELED BACK AND FORTH FROM IMAGE TO WORD TO CAPTURE ANOTHER GLIMPSE OF BASQUIAT.

MOMENTUM'S SECRET

your nose brushes
the glossy cover,
durational strides,
indignant hovering,
noble inhales held,
held into slow pullbacks,
emancipated long,
lineal sight strokes

                                      like you're reading
                                                really reading

                but what's a word (*you smirk!*)
to the one who already won the page?

                            stories-spoken, still-life hymns
                            ghostly/matter,[1] scribble/sounds

sentence runners
                    paragraph fumblers
                                      syllable jugglers

spanning   scripts   across   every   other

                                                              l   e   a   f

    rally strums in phonetic gesture

        unfollow vowels for maps, days, the dead

rooted, mystical, moved—

                                          timed register.

in the distance between truth & dreaming
you're just fog against my skin

I touch out: do I still

smell
      like
           your
                Rican
                    kid?

in the disappearance between grasp & presence
there's syntax inferred, insights omitted from archives
& miseducations[2] mobilizing the senses

      to
      crack
      open
      worlds

already
broken

broken

broken

by

lisp　　　　　s

---

1. THE MENTION OF A GHOSTLY MATTER IS INDEBTED TO AVERY GORDON'S 1997 BOOK *GHOSTLY MATTERS: HAUNTING AND THE SOCIOLOGICAL IMAGINATION*.

2. Hill, *The Miseducation of Lauryn Hill*.
   THIS POEM WAS WRITTEN ALONGSIDE LAURYN HILL'S 1998 ALBUM *THE MISEDUCATION OF LAURYN HILL*. ON REPEAT, HILL HELPED RESUSCITATE THE DEAD AND OFFER ALL KINDS OF MISEDUCATIONS FOR LIVING IN A HOSTILE WORLD, A WORLD WHERE WRITTEN LANGUAGE BOTH BITES AND BLINDS THE ALREADY VULNERABLE.

WITH WE

could we be more than residuals of colonial-racial-
capital's[1] folds
value-exchanges rolled & resold
retold, say consoled, in non-gold
commodities[2] clasped in big bucks & non-study holds
to be some-thing, never some-one, any-thing to mold
fetish cues for the brazenly patrolled
controlled upon scold, market extolled?[3]

could we be brighter than bothered & bold?

---

1   Koshy et al., *Colonial Racial Capitalism*.
2   Marx and Engels, "The Fetishism of Commodities and the Secret Thereof," 319.
3   Marx and Engels, "The Fetishism of Commodities and the Secret Thereof," 320.
    "A COMMODITY APPEARS, AT FIRST SIGHT, A VERY TRIVIAL THING, AND EASILY UNDERSTOOD. ITS ANALYSIS SHOWS THAT IT IS, IN REALITY, A VERY QUEER THING, ABOUNDING IN METAPHYSICAL SUBTLETIES AND THEOLOGICAL NICETIES. SO FAR AS IT IS A VALUE IN USE, THERE IS NOTHING MYSTERIOUS ABOUT IT, WHETHER WE CONSIDER IT FROM THE POINT OF VIEW THAT BY ITS PROPERTIES IT IS CAPABLE OF SATISFYING HUMAN WANTS, OR FROM THE POINT THAT THOSE PROPERTIES ARE THE PRODUCT OF HUMAN LABOUR."
    "A COMMODITY IS THEREFORE A MYSTERIOUS THING, SIMPLY BECAUSE IN IT THE SOCIAL CHARACTER OF MEN'S LABOUR APPEARS TO THEM AS AN OBJECTIVE CHARACTER STAMPED UPON THE PRODUCT OF THAT LABOUR; BECAUSE THE RELATION OF THE PRODUCERS TO THE SUM TOTAL OF THEIR OWN LABOUR IS PRESENTED TO THEM AS A SOCIAL RELATION, EXISTING NOT BETWEEN THEMSELVES, BUT BETWEEN THE PRODUCTS OF THEIR LABOUR. THIS IS THE REASON WHY THE PRODUCTS OF LABOUR BECOME COMMODITIES, SOCIAL THINGS WHOSE QUALITIES ARE AT THE SAME TIME PERCEPTIBLE AND IMPERCEPTIBLE BY THE SENSES."

TEN SCENES IN GARGOYLES

1.

leftist poetry teacher, former student of lowell, learner
of ginsberg, future-tense guggenheimer, committed writer
of immigrants, janitors & other red topics/people.

2.

brown student, inner street speck, black ringlets, cha-cha
intonations, $2.00 jumper & Hampton jacket, combat boots,
Lolita buttons, $ store cherry red lipstick, f*7* the 5.0 patches
& other radicalities.

3.

fran's genuine poet-students wrote like learned ethnographers, not
city youth. they spoke so damn good or was it well? chose rhyme
& meter over cleaning lady moms, illiterate dads, feeling faces of
glum-colonial-reality-presence.

4.

one Indian peer mastered stanzas on the postcolonial—cows &
Bombay folk shat near the same buses, smells slipped in histories
of British chips, fish, cheap scotch.

5.

then there were those poems of freedom fighters fran mistook for
soccer players, moments framed in magical realism & footnotes
overlooked "because good poems should never have to contain
explanations."

6.

fran shifted muzzles on brown girl's meditation poem—
enunciations in tattered accents & blues. enjambments
proudly direct. brown girl—invisibly soundless
through cotton-colored/covered mutterings.

7.

but fran just wanted to study & there's no harm in theory as
planned stanza, right? mild revolutions taped to tails, spic &
spanning through guilt-remedy & fake funk lessons.

8.

brown girl hunched at a snail's pace & rode the windpipes
of someone else's value. she imagined hustling fran
in front of her peers; shredding her poems like plath
to hughes; spitting on her *Understanding Poetry*[1] book
& landing on keats while keeping Langston resistant, dry.

9.

poetic utopia loomed low as fran imagined
the neo-independistas kicking balls around

Gooooooooool

                      Gooooooooool

                                        Gooooooooool

10.

prisoners of war & bourgeois soccer matches—dreamscapes on *el paseo Boricua*[2] where Ricans feel walking as anticolonial taps over pavement bombs.

---

1   Brooks and Warren, *Understanding Poetry*.

2   THIS WAS ORIGINALLY A MEDITATION POEM OF WALKING THE STREETS OF PASEO BORICUA IN HUMBOLDT PARK, CHICAGO, AND WAS WRITTEN FOR A POETRY COURSE ASSIGNMENT. AS THE MEDITATION DIDN'T MEET THE COLONIAL MEDIATION FOR WRITING GOOD POEMS, IT WAS LEFT IN A FOLDER FOR MORE THAN TWENTY YEARS TO REAPPEAR AS A SET OF SCENES, OR RE-MEMORY SCENES OF A MOMENT TEMPORALLY PASSED BUT NOT QUITE EMOTIONALLY ADDRESSED. IN FINDING THIS POEM AGAIN AND RECALLING THE EDUCATIONAL SCENE, I BEGAN TO TURN TO POETRY, RETURN, NOT TURN AWAY, FROM THIS FIRST ACT OF LOVE WITH STUDY. I EDITED CERTAIN MOMENTS IN THE POEM AND THE REST APPEAR AS WRITTEN ORIGINALLY BACK IN THE 1990S. AGAIN, IT IS MY TURN TO THE MEMORY SCENE. OTHERS MAY HAVE EXPERIENCED IT ALL DIFFERENTLY, BUT I HAVE COME TO KNOW THAT WHEN A STAIN REFUSES TO BE REMOVED, IT HAS TRAUMATIZED THE FABRIC FOREVER.

tURN tURN tURN tURN tURN tURN tURN tURN tURN tURN
tURN tURN tURN tURN tURN tURN tURN tURN tURN tURN
tURN tURN tURN tURN tURN tURN tURN tURN tURN tURN
tURN tURN tURN tURN tURN tURN tURN tURN tURN tURN
tURN tURN tURN tURN tURN tURN tURN tURN tURN tURN
tURN tURN tURN tURN tURN tURN tURN tURN tURN tURN
tURN tURN tURN tURN tURN tURN tURN tURN tURN tURN
tURN tURN tURN tURN tURN tURN tURN tURN tURN tURN
tURN tURN tURN tURN tURN tURN tURN tURN tURN tURN
tURN tURN tURN tURN tURN tURN tURN tURN tURN tURN
tURN tURN tURN tURN tURN tURN tURN tURN tURN tURN
tURN tURN tURN tURN tURN tURN tURN tURN tURN tURN
tURN tURN tURN tURN tURN tURN tURN tURN tURN tURN
tURN tURN tURN tURN tURN tURN tURN tURN tURN tURN
tURN tURN tURN tURN tURN tURN tURN tURN tURN tURN
tURN tURN tURN tURN tURN tURN tURN tURN tURN tURN
tURN tURN tURN tURN tURN tURN tURN tURN tURN tURN
tURN tURN tURN tURN tURN tURN tURN tURN tURN tURN
tURN tURN tURN tURN tURN tURN tURN tURN tURN tURN
tURN tURN tURN tURN tURN tURN tURN tURN tURN tURN
tURN tURN tURN tURN tURN tURN tURN tURN tURN tURN
tURN tURN tURN tURN tURN tURN tURN tURN tURN tURN
tURN tURN tURN tURN tURN tURN tURN tURN tURN tURN
tURN tURN tURN tURN tURN tURN tURN tURN tURN tURN
tURN tURN tURN tURN tURN tURN tURN tURN tURN tURN
tURN tURN tURN tURN tURN tURN tURN tURN tURN tURN
tURN tURN tURN tURN tURN tURN tURN tURN tURN tURN

PREMONITIONS: *UNTURNED*

I lend you signifiers and signs, read or unread, for brown study is more than a depressed solo endurance act completed on this material plane, in one individual scene. Brown study, in relation to brownness, is a non-exhaustive fragment full of possibility and aliveness, which binds suffering to light, which turns left to turn into something otherwise wiser than our present hostile condition.

Or brown study is curious care & compassionate listening for those here, there, all over material and immaterial terrain that glimmer & glide in visual absence and symphonic kaleidoscope. To brown study is to contemplate the past so deeply that it makes one turn, return, plan preturns for a kind of brownness that punctures infrastructure & demands the attention of precision, even if and when such contemplation drops one in the bounce of reverie.

If just one left turn returns us to brown, returns some defeat or casualty into a spoken-read for brownness, for me, for them, for him, for us-all, may the turn patch an interwoven frame over the broken. The wound is a reminder that study is mourning, yes, but it is also always alive, always un-still. Like study, categories of difference retain the gloom of their potential; in everything positioned as stable remains the residue of ongoing departure. Difference always evolves. Mourning also becomes something other in movement.

I drop you, ghost listener & spirit reader, in wondering. To wonder if what helps us sustain diverse kinds of loss may also take the form of a "certain possession of freedom,"[1] perhaps an afflictive freedom that forms friendship with the shapeless—you, me, her, him, them, us-all in

times & spaces
dynamically
unseen within
the brutal &
beautifying
confines of

difference.

---

1   Barthes, "March 2, 1978," in *Mourning Diary,* 98.

turn turn turn turn turn turn turn turn turn turn turn turn turn turn
(repeated)

ACKNOWLEDGMENTS

Many incredible folks held this text by offering feedback; listening to and reading poems aloud; responding to poem texts; helping format poems, citations, and typographical pages; guiding words into clarity; encouraging the life of this project with affection and careful attention; and becoming muse, hope, and material/immaterial chorus.

I am eternally grateful to this chorus: Laura Coby, Paulina Camacho Valencia, Issy Márquez, Trinidad Gómez, Jessica Kadish Hernández, Melody Contreras, Mark Ebbay, Lucia Cantero, Hypatia Vourloumis, Julia Steinmetz, Susan Koshy, Siobhan Somerville, Joshua Chambers-Letson, Vijay Iyer, Ruth Nicole Brown, Fred Moten, Bebe Ruiz, Alberto Brandariz Núñez, Nereida Ruiz (mami), Sofia Fey, heidi andrea restrepo rhodes, Christy Acevedo, E. Feinberg, Lauren Berlant, José Esteban Muñoz, Randy Martin, Juan C. Ruiz, Eloisa Rodriguez, Michael Rodriguez, Edna V. Fuentes, Eli, Adrian Jonas Smith, Laura Jaramillo, Ryan Carson, Eric, David Lojkovic, Michael A., Wilson Valentín-Escobar, Alicia P. Rodriguez, Rajiv Nunna, Raquel Gutiérrez, M. Laura Castañeda, s.g. maldonado vélez, Zoraya Garces, Ricky Lutz Abisla, Erica Gressman, Kiki C., Lindsay Russell, Sam Dash, Masi Asare, Kevin Hamilton, Anderson, Daniel Hughes Varnola, and Blair Ebony Smith.

A very special thank you to my fierce and wickedly smart Duke University Press editor, Courtney Berger, who took a chance on this book with great enthusiasm and care. Their feedback and guidance have been invaluable throughout the entire process. To the two anonymous Duke UP readers: I am so grateful you helped turn ideas into a text! Julieta, your stories turn words into worlds—gracias!

Big thank you to Laura Coby for reading and beautifully editing poems along the dreaming in left turns premise. Gracias to Paulina for holding ideas, tears, and verses like a pulsating heart. A tremendous gracias to Issy Márquez for reading every poem aloud, listening for the musicality of it all, and traveling the book's journey with slick turn pages and endnotes for life—and for seeing this work as a testimony to our Chicago Rican worlds. Thank you to Trinidad Gómez for hours of deep listening and rigorous care across every page—for crossing the finish line with the baton. Thank you, mami, for listening to poems over the phone and helping me honor those spirits who form and inform our everyday. To my sister Bebe, thank you for always inspiring me to write, dream, and repeat. Mil gracias to Alberto Brandariz Núñez for the sweetest love and championing, and to our Gali Lolita, who recites poetry (or howling heartbreaks) daily, and may forever hold us. Thank you for the opportunity to study and express what a janitor's kid can still spill across and shake into pages.

BIBLIOGRAPHY

Wright, Michelle M. *Physics of Blackness: Beyond the Middle Passage Epistemology*. Minneapolis: University of Minnesota Press, 2015.

Whitehead, Joshua. *Making Love with the Land: Essays*. Minneapolis: University of Minnesota Press, 2022.

Vuong, Ocean. *Night Sky with Exit Wounds*. Port Townsend, WA: Copper Canyon, 2016.

Vourloumis, Hypatia. "Ten Theses on Touch, or, Writing Touch." *Women and Performance*, February 2, 2015.

Vogel, Shane. *Stolen Time: Black Fad Performance and the Calypso Craze*. Chicago: University of Chicago Press, 2018.

Villarreal, Angelica Vanessa. "A Field of Onions: Brown Study." *Waxwing Literary Journal*, no. 8 (Spring 2016).

Viego, Antonio. *Dead Subjects: Toward a Politics of Loss in Latino Studies*. Durham, NC: Duke University Press, 2007.

Vazquez, Alexandra T. *Listening in Detail: Performances of Cuban Music*. Durham, NC: Duke University Press, 2013.

Vargas, R. Deborah. "Ruminations on Lo Sucio as a Latino Queer Analytic." *American Quarterly* 66, no. 3 (2014): 715–26.

Taylor-Garcia, Daphne V. *The Existence of the Mixed Race Damnés: Decolonialism, Class, Gender, Race*. London: Rowman and Littlefield, 2020.

Taylor, Diana. "Dancing with Diana: A Study in Hauntology." *TDR* 43, no. 1 (1999): 59–78.

Stein, Sadie. "Golden Brown." *Paris Review*, February 3, 2015.

Sharma, Nitasha Tamar. "Brown." In *Keywords for Asian American Studies*, edited by Cathy J. Schlund-Vials, Linda Trinh Võ, and K. Scott Wong, 18–20. New York: New York University Press, 2015.

Sedgwick, Eve Kosofsky. "Queer and Now." In *Tendencies*, 1–20. Durham, NC: Duke University Press, 1993.

Santini, Antonio, and Dan Sickles, dir. *Mala Mala*. New York: Killer Films, 2014.

Sandoval, Chela. *Methodology of the Oppressed*. Minneapolis: University of Minnesota Press, 2000.

Ruiz, Sandra, and Hypatia Vourloumis. *Formless Formation: Vignettes for the End of This World*. New York: Minor Compositions, 2021.

Ruiz, Sandra. "Unbodying Grunts." In "Atlas: Skin/Bone/Blood: Body Maps in Brown and Black," edited by heidi andrea restrepo rhodes, special issue, *Apogee Journal* 18 (2022).

Ruiz, Sandra. *Ricanness: Enduring Time in Anticolonial Performance*. New York: New York University Press, 2019.

Rodríguez, Richard T. *Next of Kin: The Family in Chicano/a Cultural Politics*. Durham, NC: Duke University Press, 2009.

Rodriguez, Richard. "The Brown Study." *Creative Nonfiction*, nos. 24/25 (2005).

Rodríguez, Juana María. *Sexual Futures, Queer Gestures, and Other Latina Longings*. New York: New York University Press, 2014.

Rodríguez, Juana María. *Queer Latinidad: Identity Practices, Discursive Spaces*. New York: New York University Press, 2003.

Rivera-Servera, Ramón H. *Performing Queer Latinidad: Dance, Sexuality, Politics*. Ann Arbor: University of Michigan Press, 2012.

Riggs, T. Marlon, dir. *Tongues United*. San Francisco: California Newsreel, 1989.

rhodes, heidi andrea restrepo. *The Inheritance of Haunting*. Notre Dame, IN: University of Notre Dame Press, 2019.

Reyes, Israel. *Embodied Economies: Diaspora and Transcultural Capital in Latinx Caribbean Fiction and Theater*. New Brunswick, NJ: Rutgers University Press, 2022.

Rancière, Jacques. *The Future of the Image*. London: Verso, 2007.

Rana, Swati. "Reading Brownness: Richard Rodriguez, Race, and Form." *American Literary History* 27, no. 2 (Summer 2015): 285–304.

Ramos, Iván A. "Slow Encounters: Chantal Akerman's *From the Other Side*, Queer Form, and the Mexican Migrant." *ASAP/Journal* 2, no. 2 (2017): 423–48.

Ramírez, Dixa. *Colonial Phantoms: Belonging and Refusal in the Dominican Americas, from the 19th Century to the Present*. New York: New York University Press, 2018.

Quesada, Uriel, Letitia Gomez, and Salvador Vidal-Ortiz, eds. *Queer Brown Voices: Personal Narratives of Latina/o LGBT Activism*. Austin: University of Texas Press, 2015.

Prashad, Vijay. *The Karma of Brown Folk*. Minneapolis: University of Minnesota Press, 2000.

Pérez, Roy. "The Glory That Was Wrong: El 'Chino Malo' Approximates Nuyorico." *Women and Performance: A Journal of Feminist Theory* 25, no. 3 (2015): 277–97.

Pérez, Hiram. *A Taste for Brown Bodies: Gay Modernity and Cosmopolitan Desire*. New York: New York University Press, 2015.

Pérez, Emma. *The Decolonial Imaginary: Writing Chicanas into History*. Bloomington: Indiana University Press, 1999.

Pabón-Colón, Jessica Nydia. *Graffiti Grrlz: Performing Feminism in the Hip Hop Diaspora*. New York: New York University Press, 2018.

Noriega, Chon A. "A Brown Study or a Usage Problem." *Aztlán: A Journal of Chicano Studies* 31, no. 2 (2006): 1–4.

Musser, Amber Jamilla. "Sensing Brownness: On Racialization, Perception, and Method." *Afterimages* 49, no. 1 (2022): 45–52.

Muñoz, José Esteban. *The Sense of Brown*. Edited by Joshua Chambers-Letson and Tavia Nyong'o. Durham, NC: Duke University Press, 2020.

Muñoz, José Esteban. *Disidentifications: Queers of Color and the Performance of Politics*. Minneapolis: University of Minnesota Press, 1999.

Muñoz, José Esteban. *Cruising Utopia: The Then and There of Queer Futurity*. New York: New York University Press, 2009.

Mudambi, Anjana. "The Construction of Brownness: Latino/a and South Asian Bloggers' Response to SB 1070." *Journal of International and Intercultural Communication* 8, no. 1 (2015): 44–62.

Moten, Fred. "jean-michel basquiat." In *B Jenkins*, 21. Durham, NC: Duke University Press, 2010.

Montez, Ricardo. *Keith Haring's Line: Race and the Performance of Desire*. Durham, NC: Duke University Press, 2020.

McMillan, Uri. *Embodied Avatars: Genealogies of Black Feminist Art and Performance*. New York: New York University Press, 2015.

Marx, Karl, and Friedrich Engels. "The Fetishism of Commodities and the Secret Thereof." In *The Marx-Engels Reader*, edited by Robert C. Tucker, 2nd ed. New York: Norton, 1978.

Lorde, Audre Geraldine. "The Master's Tools Will Never Dismantle the Master's House." In *Sister Outsider: Essays and Speeches*, 110–14. Trumansburg: Crossing Press, 1984.

Lima, Lázaro. *Being Brown: Sonia Sotomayor and the Latino Question*. Berkeley: University of California Press, 2020.

Lim, Eng-Beng. *Brown Boys and Rice Queens: Spellbinding Performance in the Asias*. New York: New York University Press, 2014.

LeBrón, Marisol. *Policing Life and Death: Race, Violence, and Resistance in Puerto Rico*. Berkeley: University of California Press, 2019.

La Fountain-Stokes, Lawrence M. *Translocas: The Politics of Puerto Rican Drag and Trans Performance*. Ann Arbor: University of Michigan Press, 2021.

Koshy, Susan, Lisa Marie Cacho, Jodi A. Byrd, and Brian Jordan Jefferson, eds. *Colonial Racial Capitalism*. Durham, NC: Duke University Press, 2022.

Kapadia, Ronak K. *Insurgent Aesthetics: Security and the Queer Life of the Forever War*. Durham, NC: Duke University Press, 2019.

Jaime, Karen. *The Queer Nuyorican: Racialized Sexualities and Aesthetics in Loisaida*. New York: New York University Press, 2021.

Iyer, Vijay. "Exploding the Narrative in Jazz Improvisation." In *Uptown Conversation: The New Jazz Studies*, edited by Robert G. O'meally, Brent Hayes Edwards, and Farah Jasmine Griffin, 393–403. New York: Columbia University Press, 2004.

ife, fahima. *Maroon Choreography*. Durham, NC: Duke University Press, 2021.

Holland, Sharon Patricia. *Raising the Dead: Readings of Death and (Black) Subjectivity*. Durham, NC: Duke University Press, 2000.

Hitchcock, Alfred, dir. *The Birds*. Encino, CA: Alfred J. Hitchcock Productions, 1963.

Hill, Lauryn. *The Miseducation of Lauryn Hill*. Ruff House/Columbia, 1998.

Hernandez, Jillian. *Aesthetics of Excess: The Art and Politics of Black and Latina Embodiment*. Durham, NC: Duke University Press, 2020.

Hartman, Saidiya V. *Lose Your Mother: A Journey along the Atlantic Slave Route*. New York: Farrar, Straus and Giroux, 2008.

Harris, Laura. *Experiments in Exile: C. L. R. James, Hélio Oiticica, and the Aesthetic Sociality of Blackness*. New York: Fordham University Press, 2018.

Harney, Stefano, and Fred Moten. *The Undercommons: Fugitive Planning and Black Study*. Wivenhoe, NY: Minor Compositions, 2013.

Guzmán, Javier Joshua. "Brown." In *Keywords for Latina/o Studies*, edited by Deborah R. Vargas, Nancy Raquel Mirabal, and Lawrence La Fountain-Stokes, 25. New York: New York University Press, 2017.

Gutiérrez, Raquel. *Running in Place: Poems about Institutionality*. Los Angeles: Econo Textual Objects Press, 2015.

Gutiérrez, Raquel. *Brown Neon*. Minneapolis: Coffee House Press, 2022.

Gutiérrez, Laura G. *Performing Mexicanidad: Vendidas y Cabareteras on the Transnational Stage*. Austin: University of Texas Press, 2010.

Gumbs, Alexis Pauline. *Undrowned: Black Feminist Lessons from Marine Mammals*. Chico, CA: AK Press, 2020.

Gumbs, Alexis Pauline. *Spill: Scenes of Black Feminist Fugitivity*. Durham, NC: Duke University Press, 2016.

Gumbs, Alexis Pauline. *M Archive: After the End of the World*. Durham, NC: Duke University Press, 2018.

Gumbs, Alexis Pauline. *Dub: Finding Ceremony*. Durham, NC: Duke University Press, 2020.

Gordon, Avery. *Ghostly Matters: Haunting and the Sociological Imagination*. Minneapolis: University of Minnesota Press, 2008.

García-Peña, Lorgia. "Introduction." In *The Borders of Dominicanidad: Race, Nation, and Archives of Contradiction*. Durham, NC: Duke University Press, 2016.

García, Armando. "The Illegalities of Brownness." *Social Text* 123, no. 2 (2015): 99–120.

Galarte, Francisco J. *Brown Trans Figurations: Rethinking Race, Gender, and Sexuality in Chicanx/Latinx Studies*. Austin: University of Texas Press, 2021.

Diaz, Natalie. *Postcolonial Love Poem*. Minneapolis: Graywolf Press, 2020.

Derrida, Jacques. "Introduction" and "Roland Barthes." In *The Work of Mourning*, edited and translated by Pascale-Anne Brault and Michael Naas, 1–68. Chicago: University of Chicago Press, 2001.

Cruz, Arnaldo. *Queer Latino Testimonio, Keith Haring, and Juanito Xtravaganza: Hard Tails*. New York: Palgrave Macmillan, 2007.

Crawley, Ashon T. *Blackpentecostal Breath: The Aesthetics of Possibility*. New York: Fordham University Press, 2017.

Cheng, Anne Anlin. *The Melancholy of Race: Psychoanalysis, Assimilation, and Hidden Grief*. Oxford: Oxford University Press, 2008.

Chambers-Letson, Joshua. *After the Party: A Manifesto for Queer of Color Life*. New York: New York University Press, 2018.

Brooks, Cleanth, and Robert Penn Warren. *Understanding Poetry*. 4th ed. New York: Holt, Rinehart and Winston, 1976.

Beyoncé. "PURE/HONEY." Track 15 on *Renaissance*. Released July 29, 2022. Spotify.

Beyoncé. "Irreplaceable." Track 9 on *B'Day*. Released October 23, 2006. Spotify.

Berlant, Lauren. *Cruel Optimism*. Durham, NC: Duke University Press, 2011.

Basquiat, Jean-Michel. *Riding with Death*. 1988. Acrylic, crayon, canvas, 249 × 289.5 cm (98.03 in × 113.97 in). Private Collection. https://www.wikiart.org/en/jean-michel-basquiat/riding-with-death.

Barthes, Roland. "March 2, 1978." In *Mourning Diary: October 26, 1977–September 15, 1979*, translated by Richard Howard, 98. New York: Hill and Wang, 2010.

Barthes, Roland. *Camera Lucida: Reflections on Photography*. Translated by Richard Howard. New York: Hill and Wang, 1981.

Anzaldúa, Gloria. *Borderlands / La Frontera: The New Mestiza*. San Francisco: Aunt Lute Books, 2007.

Alvarado, Leticia. "Ghostly Givings: Nao Bustamante's Melancholic Conjuring of Brownness." *Women and Performance: A Journal of Feminist Theory* 29, no. 3 (2019): 243–55.

Alvarado, Leticia. *Abject Performances: Aesthetic Strategies in Latino Cultural Production.* Durham, NC: Duke University Press, 2018.

Ahmed, Sara. *Queer Phenomenology: Orientations, Objects, Others.* Durham, NC: Duke University Press, 2006.

Ahmed, Sara. "Conclusion: Queer Use." In *What's the Use? On the Uses of Use,* 197–230. Durham, NC: Duke University Press, 2019.

Ahmed, Sara. *Complaint!* Durham, NC: Duke University Press, 2021.

www.ingramcontent.com/pod-product-compliance
Lightning Source LLC
Chambersburg PA
CBHW031502160426
43195CB00010BB/1082